Don't
Worry–
I Have
a Plan.

STEPHANIE EDENS

Don't Worry—

I Have a Plan.

a memoir

MY STORY OF LOVE, LOSS, AND THE
FAITH THAT CARRIED ME THROUGH

Don't Worry—I Have a Plan.

©2024 by Stephanie Edens

Published by Stephanie Edens, LLC , Aberdeen, Washington

Requests and correspondence may be submitted by email to: stephanieedens06@gmail.com

ISB:N 979-8-9899431-0-4 (softcover)
ISBN: 979-8-9899431-1-1 (ebook)

Scripture quotations marked "NLT" are taken from the *Holy Bible*, New Living Translation, copyright © 1996. Used by permission of Tyndale House Publishers, Inc., Carol Stream, Illinois 60189, USA. All rights reserved.

Cover design by Jeff Miller, Hatch Endeavors
Interior design and typeset by Katherine Lloyd, The DESK

To my family and friends who believed in me more than I believed in myself. You kept encouraging me through all of life's ups and downs. This book is as much yours as it is mine.

◄o►

To the widows and widowers, young and old. In the quiet of night when you feel most alone, there is One who wants to hold you and wipe away your tears. In your darkest moments when your heart hurts more than you can bear, if you listen, you'll hear the whisper of love. Holding you. Comforting you. Guiding you through your grief.

Contents

Introduction

"Don't worry—I have a plan." These were the words whispered to me mere minutes after learning my husband had died. In the very moment my world was shattering to pieces and all the air was being sucked from the earth, I was given a promise—a promise I've clung to every day since.

◄o►

Everyone has a story. Some have stories of great wealth reflecting a life of overwhelming success, while others bear stories of poverty exposing losses and failed ventures. Some tell of great adventures steeped with deep self-discovery, and yet countless others experience a life of sorrow and devastating regret. Few have been gifted a life absent of heartache and trauma, one where they are free to live with little interruption or distraction from their ultimate purpose or calling. Most people don't get to live the life they've chosen for themselves; instead, they are living one that has been chosen for them, and move through life carrying pain and disappointment.

My story, though, is one of hope. A hope planted deep in my soul before I could even speak the word with my own voice. A hope that burns within me even stronger today and has kept me alive during a time when all I wanted to do was slowly fade out of existence. This isn't a story I chose to write, but it's the story that has been written for me, and I'm honored to be able to share it with you.

◄o►

Don't Worry—I Have a Plan.

Looking back at my life, I can recount several times when I was spared for reasons beyond my understanding. When I was a young girl, my life was threatened by a man who was on trial for a crime that would result in his spending a good portion of his life in prison. My father was a witness to this crime and was called to testify against this man. The police alerted my father that the man had told them he knew my father had a little girl, and my safety was at risk should my father move forward and testify against him. I was unaware of the threat. My only concern those days was whether to play tether-ball or climb the big tires during recess. All I knew was that for a while I felt special getting escorted to and from school every day. I didn't know why I was so special, but this unsuspecting six-year-old welcomed the extra attention.

As an adult, I went in for a simple operation intended to take ninety minutes but that turned into a five-hour-long complex surgery requiring a second surgeon to assist with life-threatening complications. Once again, I was unaware that anything had gone awry. The miracle of modern medications that allow a person to rest through trauma is a blessing. People were fighting for my life, but all I knew was that I was having an exceptionally lovely dream—until someone coughing in a nearby recovery bed woke me up.

However, my first real brush with death was when I was three years old. My family was enjoying a visit with my grandparents on the Oregon Coast, and we were spending some time at the beach. I was playing near the water when a sneaker wave swept up and whisked me away from my family. My father saw what transpired and quickly dove in to rescue me. His quick thinking and action saved me from the water that had snatched and threatened to pull me into its swirling depths.

While I was too young at the time to remember the details of this event with any clarity, I've been burdened with a near-lifelong recurring nightmare. In this nightmare, I'm standing in the middle of the street facing my childhood home a few blocks from the beach. When I glance over my shoulder, I see a tsunami-size wave rolling down the street and coming straight for me. I feel the panic rising through my body, causing my heart to pound and pulse to race, taking over my senses. My instinct is to start running. I need to run away from this wave as quickly as I can. But as I try to move my legs, I realize I'm stuck. I can't move! I'm frozen in place and no amount of effort assists in my desire to flee. I'm immobile with this massive wave barreling toward me.

In some variations of this dream, I fall to my knees and start clawing at the ground, desperate to escape. Even then, I feel like I'm wading through thick, molasses-like sludge engulfing my legs and preventing me from advancing even an inch.

As I continue to glance behind me, I see the wave right above my head, mere inches from breaking over me. My heart continues to race as I realize I'm about to be consumed by this powerful churning water. So, I crouch down and pull my arms over my head in a desperate attempt to shield myself. It feels like my heart will beat its way right out of my chest. I squeeze my eyes shut in preparation for the wave to consume me. I can feel every muscle in my body tightening in anticipation of being swallowed into the water and, just as the monstrous wave is about to break over my head, the dream ends. I wake up drenched in sweat and gasping for air, every muscle aching from the tension of fear.

I'd always believed the recurring dream was a direct reflection of my near-drowning experience when I was so young. However, now I wonder if it was meant as a premonition of the crushing wave that would try to consume me in the future.

CHAPTER 1

Just a Small-Town Girl

Perfectly situated on the coast of Washington is a hidden treasure where people escape the daily grind and give themselves permission to stop and breathe in the cleansing ocean air, allowing the rhythmic sound of the waves to soothe and relax their busy minds. You don't pass through Westport on your way to another destination—Westport *is* the destination.

This little gem is my hometown, and growing up here was a gift. To give you an idea of how small Westport is, what used to be an active stoplight is now a three-way stop at the main intersection of Montesano Street and Ocean Avenue. Living in a one-stoplight town means you allow extra time when making a quick stop at the grocery store to pick up last-minute items for dinner. Running into Ted's to grab those salad fixings and cheesy rolls could take half an hour simply because you run into someone you know while choosing a perfectly ripe tomato. You can't just walk by without exchanging greetings and asking how their family is doing or how business is going. This encounter may set dinner back a few minutes, but it's moments like these that over time have built our strong community.

While Westport may be best known as a small fishing community, it's so much more than that to me. It's a community of people and, in my opinion, some of the most amazing people to ever walk the earth.

This community has been home to fishermen, loggers, cranberry farmers, small business owners, educators, and easygoing surfers, among others. Although once coined the Salmon Capital of the World, it has drawn people for far more than fishing. Many have stayed and made this their home because they, like me, appreciate the beauty of not just the landscape but the people who make it the hometown it is.

Peeking above the tops of the beach pines is a treasure we're proud to call ours. Our lighthouse, *my lighthouse*, originally provided a beacon of light guiding and welcoming sailors and fishermen to safety from an oftentimes treacherous ocean. For me, it became a sign of comfort as a little girl. Each night after my parents said prayers with me, tucked me into bed, and turned out my light, I'd then gently pull my curtains back just enough to be able to see the night sky. I'd lie in bed and watch the rotation of the light as it gently lulled me to sleep. Lying warm beneath my covers, I'd watch for the light, originally meant as a beacon to sailors, pass over my house as it had now become a beacon to me. White . . . red . . . white . . . red . . . became the familiar rhythm as I quietly drifted off to sleep. Today, as an adult, I get to watch that same lighthouse from my bedroom window each night and, warm beneath the covers, often fall asleep to the rhythmic rotation of the light as it passes through the dark night sky.

◄○►

The beauty of growing up in a small town truly is in the community of people. Those who are locals say we all know each other. While that may not be 100 percent accurate, we're all connected through our family or friends.

My hometown consists of generations of families, each with a unique connection to the other and known by the family's last name. Whether or not we're related to each other by blood, we were teammates on the same athletic team, graduated from high school the same year, or worked on the bogs, a boat, or a summer job together—we're connected. We're a community that stops to help the person with the broken-down car on the side of the road, provides a meal when someone is sick, or discreetly drops off some cash when someone is down on their luck.

Don't Worry—I Have a Plan.

Even though our community is small, it's far-reaching. There's a saying, "All roads lead back to Grays Harbor," and you find that to be very true when you're vacationing in Florida and run into the brother of your children's daycare provider. Like hearing a familiar song or catching a comfortable scent, you instantly feel the warmth of that connection because it mentally and emotionally takes you back home.

I can't recall a time when a need arose or a tragic event happened to one of us when this community of people didn't stop to help. I believe wholeheartedly this is my hometown's superpower. I experienced this first-hand when my world fell apart and my people were there for me and my children. These amazing people stopped at nothing to make sure we were taken care of. There will never be enough ways to say thank you or time left on earth to properly show my appreciation for the love and care they poured over us. My community. My people. They're comparable to none.

While I could spend days describing the beauty of my hometown, I know there's a less attractive side of living in a small town—the absence of autonomy. It can be the best part, that everyone knows each other, but this also leaves little room for privacy, and you learn this early on in life.

For example, when you're in elementary school and stick your tongue out at your former best friend, be prepared to hear about it when you get home because your mom was notified before you even stepped off the school bus. Or when you're in high school and drive down Newell Street too fast in hopes of catching air at the top of the hill, be ready for your dad to have his hand out requesting your car keys and driver's license when you walk in the front door. (That wasn't me but possibly another teen driver in my house.)

The lack of autonomy was a challenge for me. I was known as Randy and Yoyo's daughter, Scott's little sister, or Mary and Andy's granddaughter rather than Stephanie. While it bothered me to not feel like my own person, being known by my family was also what kept me in line. I was the rule follower (for the most part) who didn't get into trouble because I understood what it meant to represent the family name. I was also afraid of the consequences of making poor choices. Hearing the word *disappointed* coming from my father was more than my fragile emotions could handle. This meant I learned how to fly under the radar on the rare occasion I chose to break the rules, like sneaking a cigarette with a friend while driving too fast on the logging roads.

I didn't inhale. I didn't get caught either.

One day I took an interest in a boy whose bad boy reputation preceded him, and I realized it was impossible to fly this one under the radar. It was the end of my sophomore year in high school when I started dating Peter Graham. It was a surprise not only to me but to many that Randy and Yoyo's daughter would not only pursue but also allow herself to be pursued by this young man.

Peter and I had known each other most of our lives simply from growing up in the same community, and our families had been connected through church and school. His cousins attended the same church as my family, and the oldest cousin was a close friend of mine. Each summer during elementary school she and I buddied up to go to summer camp. Several of those summers Peter's younger sister, Jamee, joined us. When Jamee was with us, she'd relay stories about her older brother and their stereotypical love–hate sibling relationship. I didn't always care for the stories I heard of his picking on her and am sure it was because I had an older brother of my own who picked on me—I could relate to her feelings of torment. So, at that time and for that reason alone, I decided I didn't like Peter. I placed him and my brother in the same "annoying boy" category in life. And that's where he stayed for a very long time.

◄◦►

Our school district boundaries stretched over several small areas. Our school was small enough that the junior and senior high schools were combined in the same building and all K-12 was on one campus. After sixth grade, my class moved up from the small elementary school (the building on the other side of the bus barn) to the big high school building, which meant I was in the same building as Peter. He constantly tormented me, which only solidified my prior opinion of him as the annoying older brother.

Don't Worry—I Have a Plan.

Yeah, yeah, yeah, *It's because he liked you*, you're thinking. Please understand that he was the upperclassman who was always picking on everyone and teasing excessively. Believe me when I say he didn't single me out of the crowd. He was what you might call an equal opportunity teaser, and was relentless.

If there are parents reading this who are worried about their child who teases excessively and you're wondering if there's hope for someone to love them, let me reassure you to stay strong: there's hope!

In time, Peter's teasing became flirtatious—during his senior year and my freshman year. I didn't recognize or acknowledge it as flirting until much, much later. Like, a full year later.

During my freshman year of high school, Peter and I were in the band together. This didn't necessarily turn out to be a good thing for me. I was in the brass section, playing the trumpet, and he was with the percussion section playing the drums. If you're unfamiliar with how bands are situated, typically the percussion section is behind the brass section. Our band room was small, so the drummers were seated directly behind the trumpets. This meant when I played first or second chair, my head became Peter's drum set. He thoroughly enjoyed finding opportunities to make fun of me. He'd often pick apart what I wore, and his favorite prod was referring to my Birkenstocks as "Jesus shoes." He'd ask if I wore them because I was a "good little Christian girl."

In my head I'd play out a hundred different responses, but those responses would stay safely tucked away inside. Instead, I'd lean against the wall hoping it would swallow me up. I'd lower my head to avoid eye contact and pray he'd just leave me alone. I don't believe I was the picture of a good little Christian girl, but was taught to turn the other cheek and not create conflict. So, when faced with confrontational situations, I wasn't prepared to handle them appropriately. That meant the times I didn't try to fade into the wall, I shot back snarky remarks that really didn't make sense and the only response they garnered was sarcastic, demeaning laughter.

Later in the year while attending a school dance, I found myself sitting alone on the side of the cafeteria, which doubled as a makeshift dance floor. I wasn't one of those girls who got invited to dance with boys very often, so became accustomed to sitting awkwardly along the edges, watching others enjoy themselves. Peter noticed that I was by myself and walked toward me. He stood in front of me shifting back and forth with his hands in his pockets. He was wearing newer-looking jeans, which was a shift from his typical uniform of sweatpants and a T-shirt or sweatshirt. He looked nice wearing jeans, but was clearly uncomfortable in them. *I bet his mom made him wear them*, I thought.

"Hey, do you wanna dance?" he asked as he pulled a hand from his pocket and started to gesture to the dance floor.

I was shocked. *Dance with him? Is this a trap or some sort of joke? If I say yes, is he going to laugh, call me gullible, and walk away?* "What?" I asked as though I didn't hear him. Maybe if I pretended like I didn't hear, he would act as if nothing had happened and go away.

He leaned toward me and said loudly, "Do you wanna dance so you don't have to sit here by yourself?"

Oh, it was a pity offer. Perfect. That's exactly what I was hoping for. Someone who didn't really want to dance with me but just felt sorry for me sitting by myself. "No thanks. I'm fine. I'd rather not dance."

"Suit yourself." He shrugged and walked away.

I wasn't sure what to think of this exchange. This was the first glimmer of nice Peter I'd ever witnessed, and it caught me off guard. So, I couldn't be certain I could trust it was genuine. What if we got on the dance floor and he started to tease or mock me in front of everyone? I couldn't risk the embarrassment. Maybe I should have accepted, but declining was a safer option, and I would rather not have danced at all than dance with him. It wasn't the kindest reaction, but was the best I could do at that moment, and I couldn't take it back now.

◄o►

I don't recall when my feelings toward Peter started to change or even when they did change for certain. But just before he graduated in June, he was acting kinder toward me and I started to not hate him as much. I remember asking him one day while waiting for the class bell to ring what he was going to do after graduation. He told me he was immediately flying to Alaska to start fishing in the Bering Sea. I honestly assumed that was the last I'd ever see of him, and don't recall thinking about him again.

That is, until one random day during the following school year. His younger sister saw me at my locker and approached me. She had a look of concern on her face.

"Hey, what's up? Is everything okay?"

"I don't know. Peter called home from Alaska last night and I'm worried about him," she shared.

I felt a twinge of concern. "Is he okay? Did something happen?"

"He's okay," she assured me. "He told us he has a girlfriend up there and he's talking pretty seriously about her. We don't know her at all, and my mom doesn't like the sound of it. I'm just worried he's going to marry her and it's going to be a mistake. We don't know if we can trust this lady."

I looked at her and, with complete confidence, shocking myself with the words coming out of my mouth, blurted, "Nah, he isn't going to marry her."

"How can you know that?" Jamee asked, almost pleading with me.

"I just know" was all I had to offer her in response.

CHAPTER 2

P. D. G.

The spring after Peter graduated, I found myself in need of a date for the prom. Again, I wasn't one of those girls who had their pick of guys to take her to dances or even out on dates. I usually spent weeks secretly, and sometimes not so secretly, praying I'd at least get asked by one guy to go to a dance. There were a few times I was asked, but plenty of times I wasn't and either stayed home or went with a group of girlfriends. I could see this was going to be one of those stay-home-alone occasions.

I expressed my frustration and desire for a date to my close friend Andrea.

"Hey! I just got a call from Peter Graham, and he said he's coming home from Alaska soon." She suggested she ask him to be my date.

"No way. I'll go alone first."

She absolutely insisted it would be just for fun. He'd be home in time, and it would just be one date and at least I'd get to go to the dance. Everything in me said not to do it, but I wanted to go to the prom, so I conceded and told her to go ahead and talk to him. I was pretty convinced he wouldn't want to go anyway, so what did I have to lose with her just suggesting it to him?

Sometimes it cracks me up when I look back on conversations I had then and see how things worked out.

Andrea talked to him, and he agreed to go. Well, how about that? This girl had a date for the prom!

Don't Worry—I Have a Plan.

Not so fast. Things took a turn, and I was again without a date. Peter's trip home was cut short, and he had to return to Alaska. I was stuck at home by myself staring at an unused prom dress hanging on the back of my closet door. It was a gorgeous dress and felt like such a waste.

I remember the feeling of disappointment that he wasn't there to take me to the dance. Strangely, my disappointment wasn't because I'd miss the opportunity to wear the dress but because I'd miss the opportunity to go with him. I was surprised and confused by this feeling. As I sat at home contemplating all I was feeling, the phone rang. Peter was calling me from Alaska. He wanted to apologize for not being home and for ruining my night. What?! This was so thoughtful of him and added to my confusion about my feelings toward him.

I did my best to release him from any guilt. He promised, "I'll make it up to you. I feel really bad about your missing prom. So, when I get home next, I'll make it up to you." As nice as this sounded, I kept reminding myself I didn't like him. Except this other feeling kept creeping in and interrupting that old feeling of dislike. I didn't understand this new feeling and didn't know what to do with it. I spent a lot of time thinking about this shift in my emotions. I'm a natural overthinker, so when I say I spent a lot of time on this, I mean I spent *a lot* of time thinking and wondering why or how my feelings had changed so much over one missed dance.

◄○►

Months later, Peter came home from Alaska during a break between seasons, and Andrea called to let me know she'd arranged for us to go somewhere with her and her boyfriend. The prospect of being in a group made me feel a little more comfortable about being with Peter Graham, but I was still apprehensive. We agreed we weren't calling it a date or even a double date. It was just some friends going somewhere together, and this little outing turned out to be an event I'd never forget.

It was a hot and humid day, which was rare for the Pacific Northwest. So, the plan was to take a walk on the beach to a swimming hole Peter knew about from years past. Andrea convinced me to wear cut-off denim shorts and a tank top over my very modest swimsuit. Neither item of clothing was my style or made me feel comfortable. She assured me I looked good and reminded me we were just going to have a fun day. I always let her talk me into things. She was so confident in her choices, and it was just easier for me to go along with her idea than to try to make my own decision. Ultimately, this meant I was uncomfortable before our excursion even began.

We all loaded into her boyfriend's black convertible Mustang and headed for the beach. I didn't know if it was the thrill of the ride or sitting so close to Peter that made my stomach do flips, but I definitely enjoyed that moment.

I had to force myself not to stare at him. I didn't remember him looking like this before. Did a year out of high school make that big of a difference, or was it the physical labor of commercial fishing that made him look the way he did? His muscles had bulked up since the last time I saw him, his blue eyes shone brighter, and his smile felt warmer. I wasn't disappointed with what I saw.

At the beach we removed our shoes and proceeded down a sandy path. The reflection of the sun off the sand heated us quickly, and I quietly hoped I wouldn't break out into a sweat. How gross would that be?

"Hey, does anybody have sunscreen?" Peter asked as we walked the trail. I hadn't even thought about sunscreen. We don't typically get enough sun to warrant it and, even though I have fair skin, I don't burn easily. It occurred to me as I looked at this six-foot-tall redhead that he might be in greater need of sunscreen than the rest of us. His fair skin, peppered with freckles, was already showing signs of sunburn on his shoulders and cheeks.

"Oh, sorry. I didn't think to grab any. Hopefully, you won't burn. But if you do, it'll just turn into a tan, right?" I said apologetically.

He laughed. "I don't tan. I'm either white or red, but never tan."

I understood fair skin but didn't realize there was an added level of fairness with redheads. I didn't know if I was supposed to laugh with or at him over this, so just smiled and kept on walking.

We decided to drop our shoes and the car keys at the base of the dune so we wouldn't get them wet and excitedly made our way through the hot sand to the "really cool" swimming hole. When we arrived, the swimming hole was nothing close to cool. It had what looked like sewage water being pumped into it. Stinky, copper-brown water was pouring from a pipe sticking out of the ground and dumping right into the hole I was no longer willing to swim in.

We turned and looked at Peter with questioning eyes and not-so-subtle disappointment on our faces. "What the heck is this?" we all asked.

Peter stood there mirroring our confusion and shrugged his shoulders. "Huh, it used to be cool. This isn't what I remembered it to be. I dare you to jump in." He said with the old sly smirk I remembered from the past. "Or, if you don't want to jump in, I'll throw you in!"

I didn't stop to think even for a second. I just started running for the dune. I remembered this guy from high school, and wasn't taking any chances now. Thankfully, he was only teasing and nobody was thrown into the swamp water.

We made our way to get our shoes and keys, discussing alternative plans to head for the river. As we turned a corner, we looked up to see a man standing at the top of the dune, holding our shoes and car keys and brandishing a shotgun. Oh, this wasn't good.

"You guys are trespassing on my land! I've called the sheriff and you're staying right here until he gets here and takes care of you."

I panicked inside, trying to understand how we got into this kind of trouble. I turned to Peter: "Really cool swimming hole, man," I said. He just looked at me, then turned his attention to the old codger holding us hostage and tried to negotiate.

"Listen, we had no idea this was private property. Just give us our stuff back and we'll get out of here."

"No way. There are 'No Trespassing' signs posted along that pathway," he said, pointing to his right. "You'll stay right here and get what's coming to you."

"Well, we didn't come that way, so we didn't see them. Just give us our stuff and we'll get out of here." Peter was clearly trying to keep his cool in front of us, but I could see his self-control wearing thin.

P. D. G.

Thankfully, about the time I saw the muscles in his jaw flexing from clenching his teeth, the sheriff crested the dune. After a brief explanation of what had happened, we were given our shoes and keys and advised to not come back this way. *Not a problem for me!* I was thinking as I quickly gathered my things. As we walked away, we could hear the sheriff giving the old guy a warning that stealing shoes and holding people hostage with a firearm would result in much greater consequences for him next time. *I should hope so!*

I explained to Andrea later that if this was a sign of things to come, I was out. I wasn't on board with this type of excitement. I was a good girl and didn't enjoy getting into trouble.

Andrea persisted: "Come on. This was a fluke. Let's plan something else."

She could be very convincing, and I was fairly obliging (a pushover). So, I agreed to try again.

"Good," she said. "I invited him to church on Sunday. He said he'd be there, so maybe we could go somewhere after church?"

Ha! Peter won't come to church. Game over. I win.

He came to church.

When I walked in, I saw him sitting next to Andrea toward the back of the sanctuary. There was one chair left open on the end next to her. She looked at me with her Cheshire cat grin. When I sat down she leaned over and whispered, "I told him you'd be here. He came for you." Did my heart just do a flip inside my chest?

I sat next to her and leaned forward pretending to pick something up, trying to catch a glimpse of him. It was clear he'd made an effort because his hair, perfectly combed to the side, was still damp from a shower. He was wearing new dark denim jeans with a blue, burgundy, and white thin-striped Henley. I glanced down and noticed his new, never-been-scuffed, dark brown Romeos. *Nice effort*, I thought.

I was still apprehensive about him but could feel my pulse racing. I was thankful we were sitting toward the back of the church because I was quite sure it was apparent I wasn't paying attention. While I tried to sort through all the thoughts and questions running through my mind, my dear friend wrote a message on the church bulletin, folded it in half, and discreetly passed it to me. In case you were unaware, church bulletins are for far more than announcements and sermon notes. They double as a tool for conducting silent conversations with your friends.

I opened the bulletin and stared in shock at what she'd written. *He loves you.* I quickly folded it back over as my face flushed as red as the blood of Jesus the pastor was speaking of. I'm fairly certain I temporarily lost consciousness as well.

After catching my breath, I tried to sneak another peek at him out of the corner of my eye, praying he hadn't seen what she'd written. Lord, help me if he saw that! I quickly scribbled a note back to her. *No, he does not. Stop it!* I made sure I had sight of him through my peripheral to ensure he didn't see the note. She read my response and just looked at me with that same darn smile and nodded her head. Ugh, she was so frustrating.

I could see him fiddling with something and wondered if he'd seen the note, but quickly realized he'd taken his necklace off and was holding it in his hands. It was a silver rope chain with a Saint Christopher pendant hanging from it. I didn't understand why he wore it, because he wasn't Catholic or religious in any way that I knew of. I saw him hand the chain to Andrea and whisper something in her ear. He looked at me, and then faced forward, squirming in his seat. I thought that was it. He'd lasted fifteen minutes of the service and now was going to bolt. I should have known he wouldn't stay until the end.

But he didn't bolt. He just sat and continued to shift in his seat while Andrea put the necklace in my hand and whispered in my ear, "I told you he loves you." A necklace isn't a sign of love—it's simply a necklace with a Saint Christopher and what looked like *P. A. G.* scratched on the back. Who the heck was Pag and why did Peter have her necklace? Was Pag the girlfriend his sister was telling me about? That's cool. Hand me a necklace with another girl's name on it. I might not have been asked out on dates, but I wasn't desperate.

Some very long uncomfortable moments hung in the air as the pastor preached about Lord knows what. Yes, the Lord did know, but neither I nor any other teenager in the back row heard what was being said. I was only able to concentrate on the silver chain in my hand and all the questions swirling around in my head.

When church ended, I approached Peter and attempted to hand the necklace back to him.

He refused to take it. "No, you keep it and wear it."

I stood there awkwardly holding the necklace, not knowing what to say or do. I'd never been in this situation, so I asked him, "Who is Pag, and why is her name on the back of your pendant?"

He looked slightly embarrassed for a moment, his cheeks flushing bright red. "Yeah, I didn't do a good job carving. The *A* is actually a *D*, and *P. D. G.* are my initials. I was given the necklace for graduation as a good luck charm to wear on the boat."

Ah, that made sense, because inscribed on the front around the edges were the words *Saint Christopher Be My Guide*.

"I carved my initials on the back so if I'm lost at sea, they could hopefully identify me by the initials on the necklace. Kind of like a military dog tag."

I instantly recognized the importance of the necklace and knew I couldn't keep it. I shook my head and handed it back to him. "I can't take this. You need to keep wearing it." What if something happened and he couldn't be identified because he'd given this necklace to a stupid girl? But he insisted I keep and wear it. The look on his face and the serious tone of his voice made it clear to me that my friend was right—he loved me. He didn't need to say it. I could see it. And it scared me to death.

———

CHAPTER 3

Living the Long-Distance Dream

Peter came to church a few more times while he was home, and would often show up at Andrea's house when I'd spend time with her during the week. One Sunday after church he asked if I wanted to go to the county fair with him and his younger cousins Shannon and Jason. Of course, I did, but had to ask permission, and my dad was a little over-protective of his only daughter. Especially when it came to boys. I had a feeling the thought of my going to the fair with this particular boy wasn't going to sit well with him. I took my overly confident teen self and expressed my desire to go to the fair with Peter, promising we wouldn't be going alone. I really wanted to go and, promising I'd be okay, pleaded, "Dad, please, please, please can I go? Please?"

With much hesitation and concern for me written all over his face, my dad conceded and again confirmed where we were going, what time we'd be back, and, most importantly, that we'd not be alone. After giving very strict guidelines to Peter as to his expectations, he sent us on our way. Off we went in Peter's late-80s blue Toyota pickup to the small county fair with his cousins.

We had a lot of fun visiting all the exhibits, playing games, and eating delicious, soaked-in-grease fair food. Peter was a perfect gentleman, hold-ing doors open and paying for everything. Watching him interact with his younger cousins made my heart warm to him even more. Shannon and Jason brought out a side of Peter I'd not witnessed before. They loved teasing him and making him laugh, and I could see how much he adored them in the way he made sure they were having fun, saw everything they wanted to see, and did everything they wanted to do. I was thankful our first date was with them. This trip to the fair had me feeling the opposite of how I'd felt after we'd gone to the swimming hole.

At the end of the day, Peter dropped me off at my house before taking his cousins home. As we said our goodbyes, a bit of my previous opinion of Peter Graham from high school faded away.

—◄o►—

Peter and I were an unlikely couple. His personality was unique from other guys I knew. There was something special about him that was unequal to anyone else in my life. He had a presence wherever he went, and walked into every room with unwavering confidence. His sense of humor was unmatched. He was always prepared with a funny story or random punchline to make everyone laugh. While his favorite subjects were hunting, fishing, and cars, he was able to strike up a conversation with anyone on almost any topic.

I, on the other hand, was the opposite in that I was, and still am, uncomfortable in groups and lack the confidence to mingle with strangers. While I know I have a good sense of humor, I'm not confident enough to tell a joke to a group of people, and can take an interesting story and retell it in a way that makes everything awkward. My nerves get the best of me, making me flustered, and I end up forgetting the punchline to a joke or the point I wanted to make with a story. This worked well for us, though, because I didn't want to talk, and he had the gift of being able to fill the space with conversation.

While Peter had a "take me or leave me" kind of confidence with no fear of confrontation, I've always worked harder than necessary to get people to like me or to make others happy, avoiding conflict at any cost.

We were perfectly matched opposites.

We dated for five years but, because of his job, were only in the same space for about half of that time. I was devastated every time he left for Alaska. I felt as though my heart were going with him, and would spend my days counting the unknown time until his return. It never got easier. In fact, it only got more difficult as our relationship grew.

This was before cell phones were commonplace. So, Peter made phone calls either from the boat, which was very expensive, or from a pay phone in town, which wasn't cheap either. The phone calls from town were more private than the wheelhouse of a boat, though, so that's where he'd typically call from. Out in a freezing-cold metal box, calling his girl-friend, who'd spent her days just sitting at home waiting for the phone to ring. Frequently, it would happen that Peter would call when I wasn't home, and I'd be heartbroken knowing it could be days or weeks before I heard from him again. Doesn't this sound like a tragic romance?

Writing letters and mailing packages was my way of staying connected with him while he was in Alaska. This is also how I found out what some people in town thought of our dating situation. One day I carefully packed a box filled with individually wrapped notes, some home-baked cookies, and Hershey's Kisses and cheerfully took it to our little post office. I must have chosen the busiest time of day to mail it, because the place was packed. While waiting my turn, the line behind me grew longer and longer. Finally, I carried the package to the counter, and the postal worker made light conversation with me as I handed the medium-sized box full of pieces of my heart to her. When her eyes read the name on the package, she stopped midsentence.

She dropped her hands from the edges of the box, smacking them loudly on the formica countertop. The sound of her hands hitting the counter reverberated down the corridor. I stood frozen, holding my breath and waiting for the critical words she was preparing to spew. She tilted her head and raised her eyebrows and voice: "Do your parents know you're sending packages to *him*?!" she asked, her words dripping with criticism as she tapped her finger on Peter's name, which I'd written with such care.

My face flushed with embarrassment and I froze in place, too afraid to glance around and see who might be listening. Surely, the entire post office. Maybe the entire town had heard her question and understood her tone. It wasn't their business, but I knew how people talked.

I took a deep breath, drew up as much confidence as I could, and I quietly responded, "Yes, they know, and it really isn't your business who I send packages to."

She pursed her lips, drew her head back in dramatic shock, and quietly completed my transaction. I rushed home to relay the event to my mom so she could stop the gossip train before it left the station. Small towns . . .

By the time I graduated from high school, Peter and I had been dating for a couple of years. My parents moved to Eastern Oregon just days after my graduation, leaving me in Westport to attend the local college. I made a half attempt at being successful in college (I was a terrible student), which wasn't good enough. So, the following spring I moved out of state with them. I felt like I was a million miles away from Peter. I didn't want to leave Westport, because I was afraid it might end our relationship if I didn't live close to Peter's home. But I did it anyway with some encouragement from a friend. "If he truly loves you, he'll come for you," she said. I knew moving was the right decision—I needed to leave to figure out what I was going to do with my life—but that didn't make it any easier. Maybe, I thought, if I were the one leaving this time instead of him, it would feel different.

And it did—it felt worse.

It took eight months (five of which he was in Alaska), but Peter did come for me. He drove 450 miles over a snowy pass in late winter to see me. The anticipation of his arrival mixed with the worry for his safety had me pacing the floor for hours. Once he arrived, I felt at peace, like a part of me that was missing had been returned. We spent the evening visiting with my parents and he relayed an animated story of how he helped a guy who'd gone off the road at the top of the pass get out of the ditch and back on the highway. It felt so good to just be in the same space as him.

He waited until we had a moment alone, then knelt in front of me and held my hands in his. He looked into my eyes and I could see the sincerity in his. He wasn't joking around or teasing. "Stephanie, you're the best thing that has ever happened to me. I know I'm not the most handsome or smartest man, but I love you more than I could ever express, and don't want to go through life without you by my side. Will you please marry me?"

In that moment the Peter Graham I knew from high school disappeared completely, and what I saw before me was the man I'd grown to love and admire. In that moment all my fear and worry melted away, because I knew I was with my forever.

CHAPTER 4

The *Miss Sarah*

Wintertime is a significant season in our small community because it marks the start of the Dungeness crab season, which also brings a flood of memories to me more than other times of the year. Commercial fishing was Peter's and my life, and crab season was the most lucrative for us.

From day one of our relationship, our schedule was built around commercial seasons between Washington, Oregon, and Alaska. For most of our relationship, we were at the mercy of a commercial boat's schedule. Dates of departure and return often shifted depending on quotas and ever-changing regulations. Being a fishing family meant you had to understand the time commitment and unpredictability of the job. However, understanding this and being okay with it are two entirely different things.

Peter would be gone to Alaska for months at a time. Often, when he'd call I'd get excited and let myself believe he was going to surprise me and say he was coming home early, but that was never the case. He was typically letting me know they were extending his stay. I tried my best to be supportive, but there were times I failed to understand and ended up whining, complaining, and sometimes crying on the phone.

During one season his return home was delayed multiple times and I was getting frustrated. He called from the boat to let me know the trip had been extended yet again. I freely voiced my disapproval and frustration in an unusually strong tone. I directed my disappointment at the captain of the boat, who'd made this decision to delay Peter's return home. When I was done with my somewhat childish rant, I was met with an exceptionally calm "Stephanie, everyone on the boat can hear you."

After a long, uncomfortable pause, *Oops. Darn it!* A meek apology of "Sorry, Red" to the captain was all I could muster, and we quietly and quickly ended the call.

◄o►

Trying to schedule life around commercial fishing seemed an impossible task at times, as we were always at the mercy of seasons, quotas, and weather. Our wedding was at risk of being delayed when a season in Alaska was rumored to be extended but, thankfully, Peter returned home in time. Just when I thought I was adjusting to the unpredictable pattern of this life, fishing threatened to steal Peter away from another life-changing event.

Five months into our marriage, I unexpectedly became pregnant. We weren't ready to start a family so quickly, but weren't opposed to it either. We wanted to enjoy being married and work on strengthening our relationship while living some life before bringing in the responsibility of another human. I was only twenty-one years old, so waiting seemed like a reasonable plan to us. However, God had a different plan and, although we didn't anticipate it, we were over-the-moon excited. We couldn't wait to welcome our precious gift and become a family.

Peter nearly missed the birth of our son, Perry, because my due date aligned with the beginning of another season. I refused to go through this life-changing experience without Peter by my side—I wasn't going to accept that fishing was more important than welcoming our son into our lives together. After many discussions and failed attempts to divert Peter's departure (as if we could control a government regulated fishery or the fish themselves), I conceded to the fact that he might not be there. Thankfully, our baby jumped in size enough between ultrasound appointments that they decided to help him arrive early. Peter was able to be there to support me during a frighteningly difficult delivery. He was given the gift of welcoming his son into the world and for him there was no greater gift he could have received. While Peter was able to be with me for the birth, he did return to work just two days later.

The Miss Sarah

It wasn't easy being young and newly married. Being new parents and doing it all on a shoestring budget and a prayer made it even more challenging, but together we managed, and loved our new little family.

Peter's parents had helped remodel an old family home for us, and we were able to move in just two weeks after our son made his entrance into the world. My parents were with me for those two weeks before we moved in and their help was invaluable while Peter was working. But the day we moved in, they had to leave and go back to their own jobs. Sitting in the living room holding my baby boy as my parents drove away, filled with postpartum depression and feelings of abandonment, I cried an ocean of tears. I looked at the sweet face sleeping in my arms and thought, *What am I supposed to do now?*

There I was still recovering from a cesarean, partially moved into a house, and had no clue what to do with this newborn in my arms. Feeling lost, I prayed, believing God would help me through it.

He did help me. He sent all the right people, and I realized quickly that, while I was originally hesitant, moving into this house was a gift. Our little neighborhood became my micro-community. My neighbors to the east became Perry's third set of grandparents and my gardening mentors. They were amazing, loving people who would stand at the fence and visit, sharing their wisdom with me. On the other side of our yard was a couple with two young kids. He was a fisherman who was gone a lot as well, so she knew exactly what I was going through. I was able to watch her manage without her husband, and it gave me the confidence that I could do it too.

Then there was the sweet woman across the street who lived on her own in the cutest little house. In her lifetime she had buried two husbands and was an absolute wonder to me. She was always happy and smiling, and I'd ponder how she could go on being so positive in life after two tragic losses. How do you even handle losing one husband, let alone two? In my opinion, she was the strongest woman I'd ever known, and I admired her and treasured every visit we were fortunate to have.

All my neighbors, who I counted as gifts, were there for me and my children when we needed them. When Peter was gone, they'd check in on us and make sure we were doing okay. They'd share their gifts of harvest from their gardens or fresh-from-the-oven baked goods with a short visit and a reminder to "call if you need anything". For them, their visits and gifts might have felt like just a neighborly thing to do, but they made me feel less alone and cared for while my husband was away.

A couple of years passed, and I felt that if Peter didn't have to be gone fishing as much, our life would be close to perfect. Married, a toddler, a house on a lovely little piece of property in a wonderful neighborhood with family nearby. Life was great.

Just about the time I started to feel this contentment, God shuffled our cards. I was on the phone one evening with my sister-in-law answering her questions regarding signs of pregnancy and what would trigger one to take a test when I realized I was answering yes in my head to all the questions she was asking. *Could I be pregnant again? No, I couldn't be pregnant again!* Or so I thought. I'd been so preoccupied with taking care of our son and house that I'd missed all the signs.

Again, God was giving us an unexpected gift. We certainly weren't planning this pregnancy, and I wasn't sure how Peter was going to react, but knew I needed to tell him immediately. I just hoped he wouldn't feel like I did—that it was too soon and we weren't ready. When I shared the news with him, though, he was beyond thrilled, and our son matched his dad's enthusiasm with the two of them yelling and jumping wildly around me as I lay on the bed. They were unable to contain their happiness, while I lay there crying tears mixed with a little excitement and a lot of fear. I had my hands full with a toddler—how was I going to take care of him and a newborn? I felt unprepared for this addition to our family, but was also hopeful the new baby was just what we needed.

I silently asked God, *Why so soon? I wanted to wait another year or two at least.* Looking back, I can see His timing was perfect.

◄○►

When our precious girl was due to make her appearance, Peter was scheduled to take the boat he was working on from Westport to Alaska, and the trip could take up to a week depending on the weather. My due date was three weeks away, but it was possible I could go into labor any day. Standing at the dock while the boat was preparing to leave, I begged the owner to allow Peter to stay home and fly up to meet the boat later, but he wouldn't allow it. At this point, many people who don't understand the life of commercial fishing would say they'd just quit, but that's not how things are done. Peter had a job working on a good boat that fished multiple seasons throughout the year. This provided our family with a more reliable income than if he'd been on a boat that fished only one or two seasons. If he'd quit, he'd have given up a good job and would have earned himself a reputation for being unreliable. That would have made it more difficult to get hired by another high-earning operation.

I realized what I was signing up for when I married Peter and knew, even when I felt like he should just quit and walk away, that leaving his job wasn't the best decision for our family's future. So, Peter got on that boat, and I stood there trying to be brave, with tears streaming down my face as I watched them untie from the dock and leave the marina. I was heartsick. How could this be happening?

Just as I'd done so many times in the past, I wiped my tears, gathered our son, and continued to take care of business at home.

Three days after the boat left the harbor, I went into labor. Our little girl had made up her mind she was coming early and there was no stopping her. The events of that night were the perfect mixture of horror and comedy and a story that could be its own book. Peter's mom, Patty, had come over to help work on our nursery remodel, and we both had sheetrock mud up to our elbows when my labor began. My brother came to get Perry and it became apparent the situation was alarming to him, as he'd not been around a woman experiencing labor pains before. He stood in one spot and just stared at me. "What's going on? What's happening?" he repeatedly asked with a look of shock on his face. "Scott, I'm having contractions and I need you to get Perry's backpack and take him home with you."

After the third time explaining to him what was happening, gathering Perry's backpack I said sharply, "You better get it together. Your wife's going to be going through this any day and she's going to need you to be helpful."

Don't Worry—I Have a Plan.

Peter's cousin, Shannon—yes, the one from our first date—was my birthing coach during Peter's absence. She arrived and helped me get into the backseat of Patty's car while Patty jumped into the driver's seat. Shannon rode in the front seat and we headed for the hospital. That is, after Patty explained to my brother that he needed to move his Jeep so we could get out of the driveway.

I tried making phone calls to let a few people know I was in labor, while still focusing on breathing through the pain. From behind the wheel Patty kept repeating the line from *Gone with the Wind* "I don't know nothin' bout birthin' no babies." I was already scheduled for a C-section the next week with my doctor in Olympia, but halfway to Aberdeen the contractions were hitting me faster than I could process. Aberdeen had a hospital with a great birthing center, but were not expecting me, and I suddenly realized I needed to decide which hospital to go to by the time we got to the Chehalis River Bridge. Would we go right to Olympia or left to Aberdeen?

While continuing to breathe through the pain I was trying to weigh my options, when Patty demanded from the driver's seat, "Left or right, Stephanie? Are we going left or right?!"

"OOOH! LEFT! GO LEFT!" I was too far into this to think I could take a chance with another hour in the car. We made it to the hospital with just enough time for me to be prepped for surgery and, shortly after midnight, I welcomed our beautiful, perfect baby girl into the world while her dad, who, somewhere in the Pacific Ocean, had no idea something so significant had just occurred. Cell phone service wasn't as robust as it is today, so I had no way of contacting him to let him know his precious little girl, Sarah, had made an early appearance.

Months later a friend told me that a daisy chain of communication had taken place on our behalf. When I went into labor, I called one of Peter's best friends, who then called another friend who was on a boat within cell range. He told him I was in labor and to get the message to the boat Peter was on. That message was passed from boat to boat up the coast trying to reach Peter's boat and I had no idea this was happening. The day after Sarah was born, my friend Tina talked with someone in the cannery office in Cordova, which was the boat's destination. She was able to fax (yes, I said fax) pictures of our baby girl to the cannery so Peter could see a picture of her when he arrived. I was told they had her pictures posted in the office and when he walked in, he didn't even say hello—he just pointed and said, "That's my kid!"

Perfect strangers who owed us nothing and expected nothing in return, yet were members of the same fishing community, went out of their way to help relay the message and share pictures of our new baby, who decided to make her entrance during her dad's absence. To this day I don't know who was involved, but am so thankful and moved by their caring actions. This is what a true community is and if you belong to a community like this, you understand what a gift you have.

◄○►

Peter was unable to come home until Sarah was three months old. It was in the darkness of night when he was able to finally peek into her pink rosebud and white eyelet nursery at that peacefully sleeping, rosy-cheeked angel. All bundled in her soft sleeper with a pink blanket gently draped over her, he just watched her sleep with a look of complete admiration on his face. When he was finally able to peel his tear-soaked eyes away from her, he looked at me: "If she woke up right now and asked for a car, I'd go buy it."

I laughed. "You'll need to learn how to reign that in before she's old enough to talk."

At that moment as he watched our sweet girl, he realized how much of our lives he'd already missed. He decided he needed to buy his own boat so he could be home. He couldn't bear thinking of how much he'd not been a part of, and couldn't imagine missing out on anymore. I knew how hard it had been on me to have him absent over the years, but didn't understand until that moment how much it had hurt him too.

We spent the next eighteen months making plans to buy a boat. We traveled from California to Alaska looking for the right boat at the right price. We finally found the perfect one for us in Homer, Alaska. We bought it from a lovely couple who'd raised their kids working on the water, which made it special to us because we wanted the same experience with our family. This couple had one condition of purchase, and that was we needed to rename it.

It's considered bad luck to rename a boat, but we're not superstitious people, nor do we believe in old legends. Peter didn't hesitate a second when he heard the condition. He already had a name picked out. He decided the moment he met his little girl that he wanted to name his boat the *Miss Sarah*.

We had our boat, it was named after our girl, and Peter was home. This was when the hard work truly began.

◄o►

Having our own boat didn't prove to be easier in any way other than our struggles were faced together under the same roof instead of from hundreds of miles apart. The stress of owning a business in an industry that's very much feast or famine wasn't easy on this young family. As many know, financial burdens can take a toll on a marriage, and it can be several years before seeing a return on your investment when starting a business. Trying to raise a family on the meager remains of that first moderate crab season wasn't easy. So, we decided it was time for me to go back to work. This felt like a huge sacrifice to me. I'd just stopped working a year prior and wanted to be home with the kids. However, going back to work was doable now that Peter had some control of his schedule and could be with them more.

A new land development company in town had purchased a couple of businesses and was remodeling before the next summer tourist season. As my parents and grandparents had owned motels and restaurants when I was younger, I had some experience in hospitality. So, I applied, was interviewed, and was offered a job. Within a year I was promoted to assistant manager and working at several properties the company had purchased. I *loved* my job and felt as though I was handed a gift with the work I was doing. I had zero desire to do anything else and worked hard. I was extremely proud of the job I did.

As with any job, each added level of responsibility brought a bigger time commitment. I was working long hours, taking work home, and occasionally would get called back after my workday ended. It rarely bothered me because I enjoyed what I did. But it did bother Peter, and my long hours sparked many intense discussions between us. The goal of purchasing the boat was for us to spend more time together as a family, and my job wasn't aligning with that goal. We agreed we'd need to work on finding a way to reduce the amount of time I spent on work so we could spend more time as a family.

With our hometown being a seasonal, tourist town, the bulk of my work happened during the summer months. Summer was also when Peter fished for albacore tuna. He'd be gone fishing during the week and then be home on the weekends to sell fish directly from the boat to the public. This meant I was working my regular job during the week, taking orders for fish in the evenings, and coordinating with customers to pick up their fish on the weekends. It wasn't as easy as people just stopping by the boat to pick up fish. Ninety percent of the orders placed were for cleaned fish. Peter would typically get in late Friday and get a decent night's sleep before he and I would get up early Saturday morning to head to the boat. We'd set up our fillet tables and canopy and start our day. We'd spend all weekend hunched over the tables cleaning fish to fulfill the orders placed during the week. Covered in tuna blood, our backs aching, we were exhausted by the end of Sunday.

Many times during those summer months, we were unable to secure a babysitter for the whole weekend. So, we'd haul an overstuffed backpack full of snacks, toys, and activities to occupy the kids on the boat while we worked. Those were the most difficult, yet most rewarding, days. It wasn't what most people imagine doing for family time, but the memories we made were worth every challenging moment.

I know everyone believes their kids are cute but, honestly, our kids were adorable! Perry took after his dad and was very personable at a young age. A real charmer. He could chat it up with just about anybody with great ease. Sarah, more reserved and less likely to talk to strangers, was so enamored by her big brother that she just tagged along and followed his lead, making them the dynamic duo of our little fishing family.

Don't Worry—I Have a Plan.

It wasn't always easy keeping two young kids happy and entertained between the back deck and cabin of a small commercial fishing vessel. There were plenty of tantrums and tears, but we learned to be creative and quickly realized that having those adorable little faces with their sibling shenanigans kept our customers entertained while they awaited their orders. People seemed to love our family business, and we loved it too. We were finally together after so many years and, through literal blood, sweat, and tears, have made this little business work for us. I'd have those *Miss Sarah* days with those cute little kids back in a heartbeat.

CHAPTER 5

Perry and Sarah's Favorite Human

Peter was Perry and Sarah's favorite human and being with him was all they ever wanted. They went everywhere together. Whether it was hunting, fishing, going for a drive in the woods, or stopping to visit people, they went together. It was toughest on Perry when Peter was out fishing and exceptionally difficult when he was gone in Alaska for months at a time. That's why when he was home, we allowed early pick up from daycare and school so they could try to make up some of the time they'd lost during his absence.

When Perry was three, Peter picked him up early from daycare during hunting season to retrieve a deer Peter had harvested. Afterward, they stopped by my office to tell me the exciting story. As they walked up the steps of my building, I could see our son wearing the biggest smile on his face. He was covered in deer blood and filthy, but to me he looked happier than ever because he was with his dad and "got to help get the guts out, Mom." The reserved and more prudish side of me wanted to rush him inside and clean him up, but my mom heart warmed at how happy he was. I mean, really? What was more important at that moment—his happiness and the memory he was creating with his dad, or the perception of those who might be passing by?

During one elk season my parents were visiting, and while they joined the kids and me at church, Peter went hunting. There we sat listening to the pastor's message when, out of nowhere, I heard a whisper coming from behind me.

"I'm going to grab Perry. I got the biggest elk of my life, and I want him to help get it out of the woods."

I was momentarily horrified. Peter had snuck in the back during service, disrupting everyone around us, for this.

You have got to be kidding me, Peter, I thought. *We're in church!*

Nevertheless, Peter wanted so badly to share this moment with his son that I wasn't about to steal it from either of them. This is a memory I know Perry still holds in his heart, and I'm thankful I didn't allow my fear of what people thought interfere with and rob him and his dad of something so precious.

The bond Peter had with Sarah was just what you'd expect of a dad and his little princess. You wouldn't know that he didn't get to meet her in person until she was three months old. She had him wrapped around her little finger from the moment he was finally able to come home from Alaska and meet her. I'm sure this contributed to our fiery little redhead so freely challenging and testing her fiery redhead dad on so many levels. No matter what, she was his princess, and knew it.

Our girl loved it when her daddy picked her up from daycare for their daddy–daughter dates. He'd take her to get lunch or just run errands and visit with everyone they encountered. On one occasion when she was four, he decided to take her to lunch, get her a manicure, and then get her ears pierced.

"What?!" I pulled him aside with a less-than-gentle tug at his arm when I found out. "What were you thinking? We talked about this, and I told you I didn't want her ears pierced until she could take care of them herself—like when she's fifteen!"

He shrugged casually: "She wanted them pierced and I couldn't say no."

I glanced over at her sitting in the chair nearby, swinging her little legs over the edge of the seat. Her darling face lit up as I watched her fiddle with her ears, wearing the biggest smile her chubby cheeks would allow. My frustration left as quickly as it had arrived and, for the next few weeks, we battled with turning and cleaning the earrings to ward off infection. It was a chore, but a chore I'd repeat given the opportunity.

Looking back, I wish I'd cared less about the unwritten rules and what people thought was the proper way to behave and raise a child and instead been more supportive of spontaneous outings and moments that became treasured memories. "Seize the day" and all those inspirational quotes didn't come about because someone imagined they sounded good. They came about because somewhere, along the way, people didn't seize the day and wished they had. I'm one of those people.

It's so easy to look back and wish you'd done things differently or better than you had, but there's no benefit in trying to live in the past or beating yourself up or playing regrets over and over in your head. That was something Peter was adamant about. He adopted that motto from his uncle Arvid, and repeated it to me often. "Live with no regrets," he'd say. "Weigh your options, make your decisions, and move forward." I've played so many past conversations and decisions I made over and over in my head, wishing I'd said or done something differently. Remembering hurt feelings or disappointing moments that I let consume way too much space in my head and heart. We all say and do dumb things we later wish we hadn't said or done. The best thing is to accept what is. Don't dwell on it—forgive or ask forgiveness. Make a better statement or choice next time, and move forward. Dear reader, please let these words sink in. Living with regrets is counterproductive, and while I'm pretty good at doing this now, it took a life-altering event for me to truly understand it.

◄○►

Peter was proud of his kids and the little life we'd built. He worked hard to provide for us, and being that provider was a job he took very seriously. He took pride in the work he did and everything he was able to give his family as a result of that hard work. He worried about how the kids and I would be supported if something were to happen to him, but I always assured him he'd outlive me. So, it wasn't something he needed to worry about.

There came a time, though, when he insisted we take measures to ensure the kids and I would be provided for should something ever happen to him. After we had Perry and Sarah, he pushed over and over for us to get a life insurance policy. He talked about other people who were also in their late twenties and early thirties who were getting policies, and felt it was important and something we needed to do. "Nothing is going to happen to you" was my standard response, so I dragged my feet. He continued to push, and I continued to drag my feet. There was a huge part of me that didn't want to entertain the thought of getting a policy for him for fear that once I did, something would happen. He soon caught on to my procrastination. In early 2005 he gave me a very clear directive to set up an appointment for us to take out a life insurance policy. So, I contacted our insurance agent and got a plan set up that would at least pay off our house and offer a small cushion should I need it, which I was sure I wouldn't.

CHAPTER 6

April 2006

The year 2006 felt like our year. We felt like we'd come to a comfortable, more positive place in our life. Perry was seven years old and Sarah five, so we were out of the exhausting toddler stage of parenting. We were in our fourth year of owning the boat and settling well into the rhythm of business. I loved my job and felt I'd found a balance between work and home. Peter also started attending church with the kids and me more often, and he even agreed to go to a couples' Bible study with me. It wasn't that he didn't believe in God, and he never spoke negatively about the kids and me attending—he just wasn't interested in going to church himself, let alone a Bible study with other couples. I was okay with his choice, but always invited him in hopes he'd attend. So, this felt like a magical time to me.

One sunny day in March 2006, while driving home after work I admired the beauty of my home. The sun was reflecting off the water as I crossed the Elk River Bridge, creating a breathtaking scene. The air smelled like spring—that distinct crisp scent of refreshing, new beginnings. The warmth of the sun mixed with the lingering coolness of winter evenings created this picturesque spring day. I felt blessed and immensely grateful for our lives as I soaked in all the beauty surrounding me, but in an instant my feeling changed. Without warning, a dark feeling of dread bubbled to the surface. *It's all too good to be true*, it whispered. *When is the other shoe going to drop?*

Don't Worry—I Have a Plan.

I had a feeling deep within me that this lovely life wasn't going to last—I just had no idea how it was going to end. I shamed myself for not just accepting God's gift of that moment and instead turning it into something negative. I do my best to be a positive, Pollyanna kind of person but, looking back, believe that feeling, that thought, might have been planted in preparation.

◄○►

April 16, 2006, was Easter Sunday and the beginning of our anniversary week. Like millions of families across the globe, we gathered ourselves together and attended church as a family. My parents came to spend Easter with us, and we all filed in together, sitting toward the back of the sanctuary. Sitting in the back was a family tradition—we lovingly referred to ourselves as the "backrow Baptists." While this was mostly a habit, we also chose to sit there because Peter couldn't sit still. He'd revert to teenage behavior, making comments and fidgeting in his seat. I was always amazed that he could seem so distracted during the service, yet afterward could recall all the main points of the sermon. I'm not that gifted. I need to be focused and take notes, which was difficult to do when he was sitting next to me.

Toward the end of this special Easter service, he started teasing and moved a seat away from me. He took off his wedding ring and set it on the chair between us.

"Now isn't the time for this," I whispered to him, feeling annoyed but also not wanting him to get the last move. So, I saw his move and raised him one. I took off my ring and placed it right there with his and gave him a smug look that said, *What are you gonna do now?* All the while I was dying of embarrassment because I knew we had to be distracting those sitting behind us. We were still behaving like teenagers. I was twenty-nine and he was thirty-three! Would we ever grow up? I secretly hoped not.

After the service, one of the young ladies who'd been sitting behind us told me she thought we were so cute, and hoped that when she got married, she and her husband would still flirt and tease the way we did. It was touching, but I was still dying of embarrassment inside.

We returned home for lunch and an afternoon egg hunt. Peter's parents, Daryl and Patty, joined us for our late afternoon lunch and visited while the kids searched for Easter eggs in the yard. It was a lovely day. I always cherished the fact that my parents and Daryl and Patty got along so well. It was important to me that we could all be together as one family for the kids. That Easter was our last time gathering as a family, but thankfully none of us knew that at the time. We were just enjoying the sunshine and each other's company.

◄o►

On Monday we were fully back to our typical weekday routine of work, school, and T-ball and baseball practices that were scheduled throughout the week. Peter left the house early to pick up a friend and get to where they were hunting before daylight. I moved through my morning routine and got myself and the kids ready, dropped them off at school, and headed to work.

Typically, Peter would get back from hunting, do some work around the house or on the boat, and, if he had time, pick up one or both kids from school and spend some time with them. That day he picked Perry up from after-school care after dropping his things off at the house. It was late afternoon when I looked up from the front counter at work and saw him pulling into the parking lot. He got out of his truck and left Perry sitting where I could see him from the glass entryway. *Strange. Why isn't he bringing Perry in with him?*

As he got closer to the entry, I could see he wasn't happy. When he was on a mission or upset, it was obvious in how he carried himself. He wasn't smiling, the muscles in his arms were tense, and his hands were balled up in fists. *He's mad and I have no idea why.* He shoved his way through the double doors and began to question me about the boat bills. "I found some unpaid bills sitting on the desk. What the hell have you been doing? I can't trust you with anything." He assumed I'd been ignoring them and wouldn't listen to me when I offered a correction in response.

When Peter argued, he was relentless and didn't stop until he saw that you were hurt. He didn't care what he said or how he said it because the goal was to cut you to the quick and make you feel foolish. During our relationship I did whatever I could to make him happy and smooth over any disagreements we had. Only in the last year or so of our marriage had I stopped tiptoeing and started engaging in intense discussions. I believe it helped strengthen our marriage, but it certainly didn't prevent disagreements or arguments from happening. Peter was masterful at arguing. If it were considered a sport, he'd have taken the trophy every time.

I couldn't be as strong in my defense as I wanted in this situation because we were standing in the middle of my workplace. "Our bills are being paid through online banking. That's why the payment stubs are still on the desk. Can we please discuss this later at home?" I explained with pleading eyes. I looked around to make sure none of my coworkers were coming.

"I don't believe you, and yes, we'll discuss this later!" he snapped. He shoved his way back out the door and left in a storm of fury.

I silently thanked God that nobody was around in the office, but Perry could see the entire encounter from the truck. I was just thankful he couldn't hear the conversation. I prayed there would be enough time between this disagreement and when I got home that Peter could cool off and we could have a calm conversation. It broke my heart that my sweet boy was there to see it. What were we teaching him?

My drive home felt long and foreboding. I didn't know what I was going to walk into. Initially, our conversation was heated, but I was thankful when Peter calmed down and was able to listen and understand what had happened. In my attempt to work my job and manage the books for the boat, I'd missed one bill that was easy to fix. Once he realized what the truth was, he was apologetic, as he always was after losing his temper.

Once we finished our conversation we turned our attention to dinner, but something else was off. We noticed Perry was missing. We couldn't find him anywhere in the house, and he wasn't answering us when we called out for him. We ran outside yelling and searching for him with no luck. I could feel my heart racing and worry consumed me. *Where could he be?*

After what felt like a lifetime, I heard Peter yell from behind the house that he'd found him. He was hiding in the back of the woodshed. Our argument had scared him so badly that he'd left the house and hidden. Once again, my heart broke for that precoius boy. What were we doing to our children? We needed to find a better way of dealing with our conflict. We needed to set a better example of how to have a healthy disagreement. I silently vowed to find a way to get us to communicate better. We did our best to explain to Perry that we'd only had a disagreement and that everything was okay.

We were able to convince him that he wasn't in trouble, and we were not mad at each other. After many apologies, we moved through the rest of our evening without event. Following dinner, baths, reading, and getting the kids into bed, Peter and I spent time discussing a trip down the Oregon coast later in the month to celebrate our anniversary. We'd be celebrating nine years of marriage in two days on Wednesday the 19th, and while we wanted to celebrate on the day, I didn't feel I could get away from work at that time. We had a history of making plans for later and then never following through, so committed to each other to make this trip happen. At the very least we'd go out to dinner on the Wednesday to celebrate.

◄o►

I know I'm not alone when I say I'd reminisce about our wedding each year as our anniversary approached. I'd recall the planning and preparation that went into that day as well as all the beautiful details and moments of the event.

The first thing I did after Peter proposed was make a special trip with my mom to try on bridal gowns. While I set out to get something simple but elegant—and specifically, no bow on the back—I ended up with a gown that was elegant, but not simple. A long-sleeved, V-neck, satin and lace gown with buttons of pearls down the back and a train that felt like it flowed from here to eternity and, you guessed it, a bow on the back. I fell in love with it right away and felt like it was made just for me. No matter what other plans happened, I knew I was going to look and feel like a beautiful bride wearing that dress.

I didn't hold back with the dress, decorations, and so much more, because, after all, you get married only once. (Or so you think.)

Don't Worry—I Have a Plan.

We reserved a lovely church by the sea that had stained glass windows lining the west side of the sanctuary. At sunset the space would fill with romantic light. It was going to be the most beautiful setting for our wedding. The groomsmen would look dashing in their tuxedos and my bridesmaids gorgeous, while suffering through the evening wearing the ridiculous dresses and terribly uncomfortable shoes I'd picked out for them. (I'm still sorry for doing that to all of you, my friends!)

Surrounded by our family and friends with everything so well organized, it was set to be the most beautiful day. When I close my eyes, I can picture it like it was yesterday.

Our guests are seated, and my bridesmaids wait in the foyer with me and my dad. I tilt my head as my bridesmaids enter the sanctuary, and can see just enough to sneak a peek of the groomsmen standing at the altar, but I can't quite see Peter. *Darn it, the anticipation is killing me.* I hear "The Wedding Song" by Kenny G, which is our cue, and my heart beats faster with excitement. I put my hand on my dad's arm, and he squeezes it. I look at him, and he's wearing a bittersweet look of pride for the moment and sadness at the time that has passed. We both turn to the doors of the sanctuary, and slowly move our way down the aisle. The air in the sanctuary is warm. Soft candlelight lights the space and enchanting music fills the air. I scan the smiling faces greeting us as we enter and make our way to the altar.

I look up and see Peter waiting for me at the front of the sanctuary. My heart skips a beat when we lock eyes. I can see all the love he feels for me as I make my way to him, accepting my new role as his wife.

My heart still warms at the vision of this in my memory. Although my sights were set on that one guy at the front, the love of those around us filled the church and felt like you could reach out and touch it.

The wedding was captivating, and the only thing that could have made it better was if it hadn't been the rainiest day of the year. It dumped buckets nonstop all day long and all through the evening. I chose an evening wedding, hoping that when I walked down the aisle, the sunset would shine through the wall of stained glass and fill the church with beautiful colors. Instead, we had dark clouds. We didn't let it distract us from our beautiful day though. In fact, it added so much more to the memories I still carry.

Rain is supposed to be a sign of good luck on your wedding day, right? But that day was on another level. When we moved to the hall for the reception, we found a waterfall pouring through the roof! My friends were running around trying to make it better, but I simply didn't care. "Call it a water feature and tell people to duck when they come through the door," I laughed. The local paper wrote an article about our wedding and the astounding amount of rain that fell that day that said, "If rain on your wedding day is good luck, then this couple has the luckiest marriage on earth."

There are many variations to the superstition that rain on your wedding day is considered good luck, and my favorite is that the rain cleanses you of sadness and tough times from your past and marks the beginning of a new chapter in your life. Other variations are that rain signifies fertility and predicts children in the future of the couple, or rain symbolizes the last tears the bride will shed for the rest of her life. The last one reminded me of Alanis Morissette's song "Ironic." Isn't it just that?

The waterfall coming through the roof wasn't the only thing we didn't plan for at our wedding reception. What was supposed to be the guests from the wedding gathering at the reception hall to enjoy dinner and cake turned into one of the largest parties I'd ever attended. The number of guests doubled from that in attendance at the church, and not only did extra guests arrive but they brought people with them. Somehow a rumor had spread that it was an open event, and when that's said in a small town, the people show up. Free food and free fun? Who wouldn't want to be there? We decided we couldn't ask anybody to leave, so we joined the crowd and enjoyed ourselves.

Our maid of honor and best man did a superb job with their speeches, but my mom topped them both when she pulled out an old envelope she'd held onto for years. After getting the crowd to quiet down, she proceeded with the speech she'd prepared.

"When Peter was in high school, I supervised a study hall class that he was in. During one of our class times, the subject of marriage came up, and Peter insisted he'd never get married." Everyone roared with laughter and cheered. It took a moment to get everyone quieted down again.

"I proceeded to ask him if I could have that in writing. So, Peter wrote it out, signed it, had one of his classmates sign as a witness, and sealed it in an envelope." She waved the envelope in the air. "I took that envelope and labeled it 'For Peter Graham on his wedding day.' I never imagined he'd end up marrying my daughter!" She handed the envelope to Peter and hugged him, and the entire reception hall erupted with cheering.

Who would have guessed that the two of us would not only end up married, but have two kids, our own boat, and so much fun and laughter. We couldn't have planned a better life than what we had. When we were together, our little family was perfect. Life didn't always go according to how we wanted it to go and often felt messy, but I think that's just life. We didn't always have it all together, but it didn't matter, because we knew we had a gift and, in the end, made it work for us. Knowing we had each other made it easy for us to face anything that might come our way in the future.

CHAPTER 7

Three Promises

Marrying a commercial fisherman meant my risk of becoming a widow increased exponentially. According to the Centers for Disease Control in 2019:

> Commercial fishing is one of the most hazardous occupations in the United States with a fatality rate over forty times higher than the national average in 2019. Characteristics of fishing operations include heavy weather, long work hours, strenuous labor, and working with hazardous machinery.[1]

The dangers of the job and the possibility of losing Peter were always in the back of my mind. Every time his boat left the dock, I knew there was a chance he wouldn't return.

For many years while Peter was fishing in Alaska, communication was limited. It could be weeks between phone calls, and I'd spend my time worrying. He'd remind me, "No news is good news," which meant if I didn't have officials knocking at my door to deliver bad news, then I needed to believe everything was fine. Whether other fishing wives felt

---

1   "Commercial Fishing Safety," The National Institute for Occupational Safety and Health (NIOSH), CDC.gov, last reviewed January 26, 2023, https://www.cdc.gov /niosh/topics/fishing/default.html.

the same or not, understanding the danger meant a little bit of fear was always dancing in the back of my thoughts.

Peter also understood the dangers associated with his career. Even after we had the life insurance policy in place, he kept pressing me to talk about the what-ifs. What if something happened to him? What if he didn't come home? What was the plan? That sounds very wise and is a conversation every couple *should* have, but I refused to talk about it. *If we don't talk about it, then it won't happen, right?* He pressed the conversation over and over throughout our nine years of marriage, and every time he brought it up, I'd deflect and change the subject: "I don't want to talk about life without you. Let's plan a vacation instead."

He started insisting we have the conversation after we had children. He earnestly wanted to make sure I knew what he wanted and I earnestly wanted to avoid the topic of his dying.

"Stephanie, if something happens to me, I want you to—"

"Not talking about it. Everybody is going to be fine, and right now I need to go switch out laundry."

I'd always find a way to shift the topic, would leave the room, or get in the car and run an errand. I didn't want to talk about it.

He didn't want me wondering what he'd have wanted me to do should he not come home one day. It was so thoughtful of him, but the problem was that I didn't want to think about what my world would look like without him. I simply wasn't willing to finish the conversation. This went on for eight years and 364 days of our marriage. Until the day before of our ninth anniversary.

◄o►

On Tuesday, April 18, I woke up shaken from a dream—no, a nightmare. It was so real I struggled to determine if I'd actually been asleep. I was in a state of panic and spent my first waking minutes trying to convince my brain to tell my heart it wasn't real. I wiped the tears from my face as I worked to focus on reality. Throughout my morning routine, the nightmare kept forcing itself to the forefront of my mind, distracting me from the tasks I needed to accomplish.

Three Promises

In my dream, I had the kids in the car, and we were driving down the hill from our house, heading for the main highway. Somehow my car went off the road and we were all ejected out into the deep, swampy field. I was using all my strength and energy to hold onto the kids and keep them and myself above water. Out of nowhere, one of my nephews appeared with us and was crying for help, so I grabbed him as well. It was a struggle to keep us all together as I fought against the swampy mud to get us to safety. With Sarah's arms wrapped around my neck and Perry and my nephew clinging to my arms, I was able to get all of us to the edge of the water, where I could hold onto an old wooden fence post at the corner of the field. I grabbed my cell phone, which miraculously wasn't ruined by the water, and called Peter to have him come help us. Only, it wasn't Peter's voice that answered his phone—it was his chiropractor's. This was very strange because I'd never met his chiropractor, but he told me who he was and said, "Stephanie, I'm so sorry to have to tell you this over the phone, but Peter is dead."

Then I woke up.

I had a lot to take care of that day and couldn't allow this nightmare to consume any more of my time. Daylight hadn't even dawned, and Peter had already gone hunting, so I couldn't tell him about the dream until later. I knew talking about it would help me process it, but that would just have to wait. Strange dreams and nightmares were not new for me and sharing them with him always helped so they wouldn't stay and play in my head all day. Especially when they were exceptionally vivid like this one. It was as though it had truly happened.

Today, I'll just have to do my best to push it out of my mind so I can focus on my tasks. Thankfully, I was successful in that while focusing on the hustle of our morning routine so we could get to school and work on time.

After work, we decided to go out for dinner. Perry needed some baseball equipment, and I didn't feel like cooking. As we drove from our house and descended the hill toward the highway, the scene in front of me with the road and swampy field brought the nightmare flooding back to my mind. It was as fresh as if I'd just woken up. I grabbed Peter's arm,

"Oh my gosh, I had this horrible dream last night and it happened right here! I need to tell you about it."

He didn't speak a word as I proceeded to retell the dream with all the emotion I felt as tears brimmed my eyes. The look on his face grew from curiosity to serious concern as he listened. I was feeling all the panic I'd felt when waking up that morning. When I finished relaying the details to him, the car had stopped along the side of the road.

Peter looked at me and said, "That's it. We're finishing the conversation tonight. I'm going to tell you what I want you to do if something happens to me, and you'll listen."

Fear shot like ice through my veins. I was stuck in the car with no way to escape. "No, let's not do this. I don't feel like talking about it tonight. Nothing is going to happen to you, so there's no point in discussing this." Tears were stinging my eyes at the thought of continuing, and I knew he could see how adamantly I was resisting.

"No," he said, the tone of his voice letting me know he was as serious as he could be. "No. We're finishing this tonight."

I tried to keep the tears from streaming down my face. I hoped the kids were preoccupied enough with their books and toys that they weren't listening. "Peter, please. I really don't want to go over this tonight. Let's just have a nice night as a family." I turned away and faced the passenger window.

"Stephanie! I'm serious! We're finishing this conversation whether you like it or not!" He said through clenched teeth.

I wasn't getting away from it this time and turned to him: "Fine. Tell me what you want, but it doesn't change the fact that I don't want to hear it and you aren't going anywhere."

We started driving again as he told me exactly what he wanted me to do if he were to die. I listened and nodded my head unable to speak or prevent the tears from falling and, when prompted, replied with a shoulder shrug, a sarcastic "Okay," and an occasional roll of my eyes. He had it narrowed down to three things. Three huge, but important to him, tasks that he made me promise I'd do. When he stopped the car in the parking lot of a little pizza place, he turned to me. "Look me in the eyes and promise me you'll do these things."

I nodded my head in response, still unable to speak because of the heaviness of the promises.

"No, Stephanie. Say you promise and that you'll do these things. I need to know you hear me and you'll do them."

Still nodding my head, I replied with a very shaky "I promise. Okay? I promise."

"Thank you. I love you and my kids, and I need to know that you guys will be taken care of when I'm gone." He said it as though he was certain he wouldn't be around for us, and his words sat heavily on my heart.

I felt sadness, fear, and a little resentment toward him for not only making me finish the conversation but also for making me promise to do the things I didn't think I could do. Now that we'd finished the conversation and I knew exactly what he wanted should he die, there was no unfinished business. Even though that sounds as superstitious as rain on your wedding day, it's exactly what I felt at that moment.

I stared out the window and prayed against the immense fear in my gut. It was a promise to do three things, and it felt like an enormous burden at the time. I had no idea that I'd just been handed an incredible gift.

◄◦►

Peter got the kids out of the car, took them inside the restaurant and gave me a moment to pull myself together. I needed a minute to replay the conversation in my head and try to process all he'd said. I also needed a minute to let my eyes dry, so I didn't walk in looking like we'd just had the worst conversation of my life, which is what I felt. *I hate that he made me finish the conversation. Now what?*

I did my best to push it all out of my head so it wouldn't prevent us from having an enjoyable family dinner. Occasionally, he'd look at me and we'd have a nonverbal exchange of "Don't forget what you promised me" and "I know. I promised. I get it." We had a fun dinner and were able to get the baseball gear we needed before heading home. Thankfully, our boy was in rare form and had us in stitches all the way home. He loved making people laugh, and was very successful at sending his family into hysterics that night.

Don't Worry—I Have a Plan.

By the time we got home, it was time to start our bedtime routine. I'd pushed Peter's words from my mind by convincing myself I'd never need to recall them again. So, no need to let them ruin my entire night. I focused on getting the kids ready for bed and preparing what was needed for the next day. It was a school night, and typically we were strict with bedtime. This night felt different. Maybe it was the heaviness of the conversation that made me want to bend the bedtime rules or maybe all the talk about death emotionally exhausted me. But after their bath, the kids stayed up a little longer and snuggled up with Peter on the sofa and watched TV. All cozy in their pajamas, they fell asleep, each of them safely wrapped in their dad's arms. I couldn't imagine a better way for them to have ended that day.

CHAPTER 8

—————

Grief

Death is a peculiar thing. It takes what's most precious in your life and rips it away without your permission. But before it leaves, it touches every part of you, affecting not only how you feel in that moment, but adding a landmark, changing how you measure everything from that moment forward. By the time you realize all the ways in which you've been changed by its touch, it's too late. You can't go back. You can't choose to be who you were before. That person is gone, and you can't bring them back. You want to go back, and you try, but death has permanently altered your emotional DNA. In time, you begin to see the way you approach life has also been permanently altered by this tragically defining moment. You realize you've come to a place where you're forced to make a choice. You can choose to stay in the moment death darkened your door, allowing it to keep its shadow hovering over you and clouding your mind and heart, or you can acknowledge its presence, force it to take a back seat, and continue to live the life you've been gifted.

I recall my first experience with death when I was a young child. My grandfather passed away unexpectedly. I was awakened from sleep by the sound of my mom crying in my parents' bedroom down the hall. I didn't know why she was crying and hearing her frightened me, so I stayed frozen in bed with the covers pulled up under my chin, afraid of what might be happening. I waited for what felt like an eternity until my dad quietly entered my room, sat on my bed next to me, and told me my grandfather had passed away in his sleep. He explained to me that my mom was very sad. I understood sadness. I felt sad, but when I saw my mom later that day, the sadness I felt and thought I understood didn't match what I saw on her face. What she wore was much greater than sadness, but my third-grade mind was unable to discern grief as a deeper feeling than sadness.

When one of my elementary school friends lost her battle with leukemia, I heard the adults telling each other she was in heaven now and wasn't sick anymore. I knew heaven was supposed to be a wonderful place, so didn't feel sad if that was where she was. If she got to be in heaven and wasn't sick, I was confused as to why that was a sad thing. I remember attending her funeral and seeing sadness on all the faces. I wondered if something was wrong with me because I didn't think my sadness matched the depth of what I saw on the faces around me.

I've carried the belief throughout my life that if someone dies and goes to heaven, they're better off than those of us left here on earth. So, when someone passes away, I struggle with feeling the depth of grief many around me portray. I'm sad for myself because I can no longer be in the same space as the person, but am not sad for them if where they went is far better than where we are. Some may think I'm wrong in this, but I believe we're all allowed to grieve in our own way.

I've had plenty of opportunities to mourn the loss of loved ones and others who've been dear to my heart, but there have been few whose passing has made my heart hurt deeply, and only one whose death has broken it to pieces with the fear it could never be made whole again.

CHAPTER 9

Don't Worry—
I Have a Plan

Wednesday, April 19, 2006, 4:00 a.m. *What's that sound? The alarm clock. Why is the alarm clock going off this early? Oh, Peter is going turkey hunting.* Rolling over and reaching out to give him a gentle nudge. "Hey, your alarm is going off." All I hear is a tired grunt in response. "Pete, your alarm is going off. Time to get up if you're going to get to Kenny's on time."

He's waking up, moving around, stretching, and adjusting to get out of bed. I'm rolling over and keeping my eyes closed. I hope he isn't too noisy getting ready. I really don't want to wake up yet. I'm still so tired. I hear him getting dressed and heading to the bathroom. Oh, please keep the bathroom door shut while the light is on. If that light comes through, I'll be awake.

"Hey, Steph, I'm heading out." I must have fallen back asleep. He's standing above me kissing me on the forehead. I reach up to hug him and say without opening my eyes, "Be safe."

"I will. Happy anniversary. I'll see you later this evening when I get back and we'll go to dinner."

Oh, yes, our anniversary. Dinner will be nice. He's tiptoeing toward the bedroom door, and I reach out and ask for one more hug before he leaves. I can hear him smiling as he walks back and hugs me. I hold on for an extra moment. "Be safe. I love you."

Don't Worry—I Have a Plan.

"I love you too." He heads out the door, closing it quietly behind him. Mmmm, I can go back to sleep and get a good thirty minutes or so before I need to get up.

The phone is ringing. *Why is the phone ringing this early in the morning?* Wait, the phone is ringing. *Dang it—it's going to wake up the kids. Ugh!* It's still dark and I can't seem to get my bearings to even know where the cordless phone may be. I'm feeling my way from the bedroom to the kitchen to answer the phone on the wall. *Oh, please don't wake up the kids this early!* I'm fumbling for the receiver, glancing at the stove to see it's not even five o'clock yet. I say hello, but am still not fully awake. The voice on the other end is trying to tell me something, but it doesn't make sense.

"It will be okay. Jacquie will come to sit with the kids."

What? Jacquie who, and why would someone come to be with the kids? I'm not understanding, and I can't get the words coming through the phone to register and make any sense to me.

"I don't know what you're talking about. Jacquie who? Why are you telling me this and who are you?" I start to feel myself waking up a bit more. Oh, I know who this is. It's Kenny's girlfriend, but I still don't understand why she's calling me this early or why she's saying someone is coming over. Is she talking about a babysitter for dinner? *Ugh.* I can't wake up enough to think clearly. I can hear the familiar tone of call waiting. Another call is trying to get through. Someone else is calling now? What in the world is going on?

I can't understand what this person is saying. So, I just interrupt: "Hey, I have another call coming in. I'm sorry, but I have to go." She's still trying to tell me something, but I don't understand. So, I'm just going to answer the other call. I click the button to pick up the other call, and hear the instant panic in Kenny's voice. Every sense of my being jerks awake.

"Stephanie, he's not moving. I don't know what happened. The truck went off the road and he's not moving. I tried to get him to move, but he's not moving!"

My blood runs cold and my heart is racing. "What do you mean he's not moving?"

The panic and sheer terror in his voice are bone chilling. "I can't get him to wake up. He won't move, Stephanie!"

No, oh God, please no. The other phone call is making sense now. I start pleading with him to tell me what he's talking about because he can't be right, but can't hear him because my head is spinning. Everything is starting to close in on me. I don't understand. I don't want to hear this. He's wrong. He must be wrong. *No, no, no, no, no.*

I have to go. I have to get to him. I hear Kenny talking still, but can't understand it. I can't. I have to go. I hang up and run to find the cordless phone. I have to call someone. Peter's parents. I have to call Daryl. He'll come get me and we can go together. I'm calling their number and it's ringing and ringing and ringing. I know Patty is at work and Daryl unloaded a ship last night. I know he's home. *Please pick up.* No answer. I hang up and dial again. It's ringing and ringing and ringing. *Pick up, pick up, pick up. Please pick up!* He's not answering. Did he not take the phone in the bedroom with him? Maybe he fell asleep in the living room. Hang up and dial again. Ringing . . . ringing . . . ringing. Why isn't he answering?

What's that sound? Why do I hear yelling? Who's yelling? I realize as I'm pacing in the bedroom with the phone that I'm hearing my own voice yelling out to God, begging Him to please not let this be. "Please don't let him be gone. Please, God, please! Don't take him from me!"

Daryl is still not answering. What am I supposed to do? *Who do I call? Who do I call?* Scott. I'll call Scott. He won't be up yet. *Oh, please answer.* I dial my brother's number and it rings. It rings again and again and finally, "Hello?" Oh, thank God, my sister-in-law.

"Trisha, it's me. There's been an accident. It's Peter and I need Scott to come and get me. I don't know what to do." I can hear her waking up Scott as she echoes the terror in my voice.

"It's your sister. You need to hurry and get dressed because Peter's been in an accident, and she needs you." I can hear panicked movement in the background and Trisha telling me it will be okay. That Peter will be okay and Scott's on his way.

Peter's not okay. I can feel it. I know her words are meant for comfort, but can't stop long enough to feel it. I need to figure this out. I need to figure out how to get to him and not get the kids up. I don't want them to know what's going on. *Oh, Lord, how do I do this?*

I need to get dressed before Scott gets here. I grab some jeans and struggle to get them buttoned. Why are there buttons anyway? So dumb. Stupid buttons! I grab my Englund Marine hoodie. I need a bra. Why do I even care about that right now? What if I end up sitting in the hospital all day? I need a bra. Oh, what am I going to do? God, please help me! *He's gone. Peter's gone.* No! Stop thinking like that. Stop being dramatic.

I can feel in my heart he's gone, and feel my world darkening. *No, focus on what you need to do next.* Brush my teeth. I need to brush my teeth. I grab my toothpaste and catch a glimpse of myself in the mirror, and the fear in my eyes is reflecting at me as I feel it morph into full panic. *Pull yourself together, Stephanie. You'll get to him, and things will be okay. It was an accident, and it can all be fixed.*

I hear someone at the door. Scott is here already? That was so fast. I spit out the toothpaste and run to the door, trying to figure out what to do with the kids because they're still asleep upstairs. I can't wake them up. I'll have Scott stay here and I'll go to where Kenny said the truck went off the road. Yes. That will work. That's what we'll do.

I get to the door and our friends Roxy and Steve are standing there. No. No. Oh no, no, no, no, no . . . I back up as they walk in. Steve is silent, but his face is telling me everything. I can see what I already know in my heart in the way he's looking at me. *Don't look at me like that.* Roxy is talking, but I can't register what it is because my brain is still trying to deny everything that's going on. What's she saying to me about the kids? I keep trying to back away from them, as if keeping my distance will keep the reality of what they know away from me.

Who called them? How did they know to come? I'm telling them my brother is coming over, and Roxy is telling me they're here to sit at the house with the kids. I think I'm explaining to her what I'm doing, but can't hear the words I'm speaking. Maybe I'm not saying anything and just think I am. Headlights. I see headlights coming up the road—it must be Scott. I explain that the kids are sleeping and I hope they stay asleep, but I'll call and let them know what's going on. Oh, the look on their faces reflects what I know in my heart. They already know what's going on, and the tears in Roxy's eyes are too much. I need to leave. I need to go to Peter and sort this out.

I grab my purse, rush out the door, and beat Scott to the driveway. I grab the door handle and it's locked. He's struggling to get it unlocked, and I can see the stress on his face grow stronger as he hits all the buttons on the door. I hear it unlock, open the door, and fall in. While fighting with the seatbelt, I tell him Roxy and Steve are in the house and give him directions of where we need to go. Then I just watch through the windshield as we race out of the neighborhood. I can't tell if he's talking or if we're riding in silence.

As we drive down the hill, my nightmare comes rushing back to my mind. *He's gone.*

We get on the highway and drive in silence. As we approach a gas station, Scott is apologizing profusely, but needs to stop for gas. He keeps apologizing, and I'm trying to tell him it's okay and give him my debit card to pay, but he won't take it. All I can do is just stare through the windshield as he gets out of the car. Peter can't be dead. This can't be happening. No, we'll get there, and he may be injured, but we'll just go to the hospital and things will be okay. He may have to take some time off, but it's spring and crabbing is slower right now. It will be okay.

My heart whispers, *He's dead.*

No, he's not. Stop being so dramatic. He's going to be okay. He's going to be banged up, but he'll be okay.

He's dead.

Scott jumps back in the car and I can feel his eyes studying me, trying to decide if I'm okay or not. He's trying to figure out what to say. How to make it better. How to fix it. "We'll get there, and things will be okay."

I know it's not going to be okay, but how do I tell him that? He sounds so hopeful. All I can do is look at him and say, "Okay, okay." We drive on and I stare out the windshield, wringing my hands, afraid to move any other part of my body. I can't move.

There's the state park . . . the Presbyterian church . . . the Christian Center . . . Pomegranate gift shop. We keep driving. The Local Tavern

. . . the Lutheran church . . . the Local Store. Where are they? Scott asks how far down the accident is. I don't know, but tell him to keep driving because we have to be close. Then, oh, there are lights. Emergency vehicle lights getting closer. We're here. I don't know what to think. I can't make out what's going on. There are so many lights, and I see people standing to the right in the convenience store parking lot.

"Oh my gosh, oh my gosh! That's his truck?!" Panic consumes me. That's his truck, but that can't be right. I can't rationalize what I'm seeing. It looks like his truck is standing on its front bumper with the bed in the air. That can't be right. All I see are tires and axles and, oh my gosh—this is bad. This is so bad. My heart is in my throat, and I feel weak. There are so many lights. Why so many lights? And people. How can there be a crowd of people already? My eyes are picking out faces. Faces of friends and other people I know. How did they get here so fast?

They know. I can see it all over their faces. They know he's gone, and as I look through the group and try to make eye contact, they all look away. They won't look at me. They know and they don't want to look at me.

I can hear Scott telling me he's parking the car and he's going to find out what's going on. The car stops and he gets out and disappears across the street. I get out of the car and walk across the street, trying to find someone to tell me what's happening. I can't feel the ground under my feet, but know I'm moving. There are so many lights, it's hard to see what's happening. I know most of the fire and paramedic crew because it's such a small community, yet don't recognize anybody. I see Scott go around an ambulance to my left, but can't find anyone I know who'll talk to me. I can't make sense of the chaos. Where's my husband? There are so many lights and people, and I can't find anyone who'll talk to me. Where's Peter? Why won't anybody talk to me?!

There's a fireman. I'll get to him and ask him what's going on and he'll tell me. No, he looked down and walked away. Maybe he didn't see me. There's so much going on, I'm still having trouble making sense of what's happening. There's someone. I don't know who he is, but he's wearing a fireman jacket and is just standing there. So, I'll walk over and talk to him. "I'm Stephanie, Peter's wife. He was driving the truck and I don't know where he is. Can you tell me where he is?" He's just staring at me like I'm not making sense. Maybe I'm not. Maybe he doesn't understand. I ask him again and he just stands there staring at me, blinking his eyes and backing away, like I'm a leper and he's afraid to be near me.

It feels like minutes are passing as I stand in front of him, pleading. How long have I been standing here waiting for an answer? I can't take it. I need to know what's going on. Nobody is talking to me, so I grab him by the collar of his uniform, and hear a feral sound coming from my mouth as my face is inches away from his. "WHERE'S MY HUSBAND?" I'm staring him down like a tiger ready to rip his timid little face off while waiting for an answer.

He gulps and, with eyes portraying the fear of a frightened child, takes a deep breath and whispers timidly, "I'm sorry, but he's dead."

Silence.

Darkness.

The lights have disappeared, and I can't hear anything. All the air has been sucked from the earth. Everything has stopped. The world has stopped.

I don't know how long this moment lasts, but as I slowly peel my fingers from his collar all I can hear is absolute total silence, and then the unwelcome, deafening sound of my heartbeat pulsing in my ears. I look him in the eyes and can see he's unprepared to be the one delivering this news to me. For a second, I feel pity because I can sense that my life isn't the only one that has changed in this moment.

I feel myself slowly backing away from him with a feeling of complete disbelief. How could he just say those words to me? How could he just confirm for me my worst nightmare and not have anything to follow it up with? How dare he?

In an instant, I snap back to the reality of the moment and realize I need to find Scott. Where is he? Where did he go? I need to find him and tell him what's happened. The lights are still flashing in my face and the noise from all the activity is making it more difficult for me to understand the words that just assaulted me. The noise is deafening. Where is he? I keep searching but can't see him anywhere. Looking to my left I see an ambulance and the back is open. Maybe that kid was wrong. Maybe that person in the ambulance is Peter. I walk over and can hear Kenny talking. It's not Peter. Scott comes around the corner. "It's okay. He's in the ambulance and they said he's going to be okay."

I look at him and see his desperate need to make things better for me. It's all I can do to get the words out of my mouth in a whisper: "That's not Peter. That's Kenny. Peter's dead. He's dead."

Silence again. Scott is shaking his head and his mouth is moving, but I can't make it out. What's he saying? I feel weak.

Someone in a uniform comes over and talks to Scott and then points in the direction of an ambulance. I can feel Scott's arm around me as we start walking. We're walking to the back of the ambulance meant to care for Peter, and get in. I'm so confused about why we're doing this. Why do I need to be in an ambulance? Am I having a heart attack? Is something wrong with me and they're taking me somewhere in the ambulance? Scott sits me down on the bench and I see him grab the phone and dial it. I'm looking out the window of the ambulance and see the crowd of people across the street staring at me. Why are they there? Why do they have to stare at me? Why can't they just go away? I feel myself getting frustrated that they were here first and just keep standing there watching with those blank stares. I want them to stop staring and go away.

I ask Scott who he's calling.

"Mom and Dad."

Oh.

I hear him start talking. "Hey, it's me. There's been an accident, and, um . . .". *Dear God, what do I do? Why? Why is this happening?* All the sounds around me fade to a low murmur, like a TV left on in the other room. I can hear Scott's voice, but it's just muffled noise from far away. Out of the background noise comes a clear, undeniable voice.

Don't worry - I have a plan.

Peace washes over me. Then the voice fades, and all the noise comes back to the normal, overwhelming volume.

I look at Scott as he's hanging up the phone and all I can say is, "We have to go. I have to go home." The confused look on his face tells me he didn't hear what I heard, because he's asking me if I really want to go, or do I think I should stay.

"It's okay. There's nothing here for me and I need to get home before the kids wake up."

He walks me to his car and opens the door to let me in and the people are still staring. I can feel them watching me and I wish they'd stop! At least I know now. There's a plan. I need to get home. I need to be there for the kids. What am I going to tell them? I've no idea how I'm going to tell them what's happened, but need to go home to be there when they wake up.

I know the car is moving, but can't feel anything. Everything is silent and dark, and I'm numb. I can't look at my brother. My poor brother. He's being so strong for me, and I can't even look at him. We pull up to the house. How did we get here so fast? How am I going to tell the kids? I know I get to the door somehow, but don't remember walking from the car. I go inside and see Steve sitting on the sofa next to the basket of laundry I intended to fold before work this morning. I look to the kitchen and see Roxy standing at my sink doing my dishes with tears streaming down her cheeks. There are so many tears.

"Roxy. You don't need to wash my dishes."

She turns to me and wipes some tears away. "I need to do something." Then she reaches out and grabs me into a hug, and all I can do is cry. The first tears. They've started. Will I have enough tears? I can't cry right now. I need to be strong. I need to figure things out. I turn and see Scott talking, and he stops and tells me Mom and Dad are on their way. Then he asks me what I want him to do. "Someone needs to tell Patty and Daryl. Daryl didn't answer their phone, but I can't tell him this over the phone. Patty is at work. Can you go get her?" I've no idea the weight of the devastating task I've just asked him to do, but he tells me he'll do it and leaves to go find Patty.

I know the kids will be waking up at some point soon, and still don't know what to tell them. How do you tell your kids their daddy is gone forever? How do I look at their darling faces and tell them something they won't understand? I don't know what to do. I'm looking around the house and noticing small details of my home that have just been torn apart. Our family photo on the wall, our wedding photo on the end table, and his coat hanging on the hook above his boots by the entryway. This house will never be the same again.

What do I do with myself? I'm just standing here frozen in place, not knowing what to do. I don't want the kids to wake up yet. I don't want to destroy them any sooner than I have to. *Please, God, let them sleep in. Let them rest not knowing what's happening to them right now.* I hear Steve say something to me and see him leave out the front door right after Scott. Roxy is still standing at my kitchen sink with tears running down her cheeks as she looks at me.

I look around again and notice the laundry basket with mismatched socks. Socks. I can sort socks. I sink to the floor and grab some socks from the basket. I can hear the clatter of dishes and water running in the kitchen, but they sound far away as I stare at the socks in my hands. Do these socks match each other? I look out the window and see daylight brimming and know the kids will be waking up soon. I don't know how to tell them what has happened.

The sound of the front door opening brings me back to the moment, and I see Daryl striding toward me. Oh, the pain and panic on his face. I look at him coming toward me and can't tell if I'm even breathing. I can't get any words to come out of my mouth, and even if I could, I wouldn't know what to say.

"Patty's in the car. We're driving down there and will figure this out." Figure what out? He's dead. There's nothing to figure out. Daryl leans down, kisses me on the forehead, turns around, and goes out the door just as quickly as he came in. Daryl has never kissed me on the forehead. This small action is more than my heart can handle—I drop the socks to the floor and start sobbing. I'm willing myself to not cry out loud because I don't want to wake up the kids. *Please, God, let them sleep for as long as possible.*

Through my tears I look at the socks around me and still don't know if they match each other. I hear the door again and, when I look up, see the pastor and his wife. No. I don't want them here. They'd only be here if this nightmare is true. Their presence forces me into the present moment, and everything rushes back. I know they're talking to me, but can't hear their words. I see their mouths moving, but don't know what they're saying. I think I'm inviting them to sit, and sit down on the sofa. Are there more people here? I see and hear people coming to the door. I look up and see my parents coming in. How did they get here so quickly? What time is it? The kids. All this noise will surely wake them up.

Pastor is talking to me, and I think he's trying to speak pastoral care and concern, but can't quite make sense of any of it. I hear him say, "We're going to go to the store to get some food for you." I thank them and tell them I have food and we're okay. "I know you have food for you, but people will be coming by. Let's get some things for you and the kids and people when they visit. How about some chicken and maybe a veggie platter?"

Oh. People will be coming. Of course, they'll come. What am I supposed to say when they do come? I look at Pastor and for a moment contemplate telling him not to get anything and maybe people won't come and none of this will have happened. Instead, I whisper, "That sounds fine. Thank you." I don't know what my face is saying, but they look like they're tiptoeing around in fear that I might shatter like fragile glass. I feel like I might.

I hear a creak in the floor from upstairs. The kids are up. "The kids are up. I need to take care of them by myself." I blurt out as I catapult myself from the sofa, push between my parents, and make it halfway up the stairs as my son is coming around the corner from his room.

"Hey, buddy." I scoop him up and take him back to his room. I set him on his bottom bunk bed and sit down with him, pulling his comforter back up around his shoulders. His sleep-filled eyes look up at me, reading the expression on my face. How do I get the words out? How do I destroy his world and convince him that everything will still be okay when I don't believe it myself?

I pull him close and hold his little hands in mine and look at his precious face. He looks confused, and I'm sure my face is saying more than my words can express. "Perry, something happened this morning when your dad went hunting." *Oh God, help me get through this.* "His truck went off the road and crashed into a tree." My chest is so tight I can barely breathe. "Oh, buddy, I'm so sorry. Your daddy died in the accident, and he won't be coming home." I can hardly make out his face through the tears in my own eyes, but I reach for him and hold him close as we rock together on his bed.

I can hear Sarah waking up, so grab Perry and take him to her room, where we sit together and I tell her what happened. I can see in her eyes she doesn't understand. Of course, my dear five-year-old doesn't understand. *I* can't even understand.

I beg God to help me through this moment with my kids. I beg with everything in me to help them and spare them. I use all the love and gentleness I can muster to explain what happened and how we, the three of us, are a family and will always be a family. We sit upstairs as I just hold them and mourn.

◄○►

We're interrupted by the sound of people downstairs, and the kids want to know who's here. I don't want to go downstairs. I don't want to take the kids down with all those people. I feel like I'd be parading them in front of a crowd. An audience waiting to observe how they're reacting. I want to keep them up here where I can protect them and shield them from all those sad people who will pour their grief all over them. I want to keep them upstairs until everyone goes away and I can just help them through this on my own. We're a family now. Just the three of us. I'm all they need.

"There are a lot of people downstairs who are here for us. They're all very sad about your daddy and will want to see you and hug you, but you don't have to let them. You let me know when you're ready to go down and we'll go together, okay?"

The kids hear familiar voices, and they want to go downstairs, so I scoop up my little girl and hold my little man's hand and we descend the stairs together to face those who await us. More confirmation of my new reality.

Don't Worry—I Have a Plan

There are new people with more sadness and their own feelings and need to take care of me and the kids and I don't want them to. They want to hold the kids and I don't want them touching them. I feel the need to keep a hold of them and not let anyone near them. They're clinging to me, so I hold them close as we sit on the sofa. My mom comes over to get the kids, and I find myself grabbing them and holding them tighter. *Don't touch them. They're mine and I'm not letting go of them. Ever.* I know she sees the panic in my eyes—she pats us and steps away. *Maybe we can just sit here together until everyone goes away and this will all just be a bad dream. I had a bad dream just like this two nights ago. I'll wake up from this one too. Please, God, let me wake up from this one.*

I know there are more people in the house, but can't keep track of who they are. Someone comes through the door holding a large bouquet of lilies. "Flowers just arrived for you and the kids, Stephanie." I look at the clock—it's only a quarter to eleven. He has been gone less than six hours. How did this happen so quickly? Flowers mean this is real and people know. These flowers make me feel a sense of finale that takes my breath away. I want them to be taken away. I don't want any flowers. I don't want what they symbolize.

"Who sent those?"

"They're from Mark, Ande, and the Towle family."

Oh my gosh, they know. People know. That was so fast. I'm not ready for everyone to know.

Scott is back. I ask my mom to take my spot with the kids so I can go into the other room and talk to my brother. Scott tells me he was able to find Patty, took her home to Daryl, and then went home to be with Trisha for a bit. He asks me if he can do anything else for me. I find myself asking him to deliver the payment for the past-due boat bill. I grab it off my desk and hand it to him. He's looking at me with total confusion. Have I gone mad?

"Really?" he says, mildly irritated. "You really want me to take care of this right now? Can't this wait a couple of days?"

I'm trying to explain to him how important it is to me because this is what caused my and Peter's last argument. I need it to be taken care of. In my head, I know how silly this sounds to be worrying about a stupid bill at this moment, but I need this to be done.

"Please, Scott. Can you please just do this?"

He looks at me and shakes his head. "Of course. I'll take care of it." He heads out the door with the envelope in hand. I feel better knowing that's being handled. It feels like being able to smooth over the last thing that upset Peter, and I can keep the peace.

There are so many people here and the flowers keep arriving and I don't know what to do. I don't even know what time it is. Oh, it's almost noon. He's been gone for almost seven hours.

My dad is standing in the kitchen, looking at me through tear-swollen eyes and holding my phone against his chest. He's signaling for me to come over. He whispers, "Someone is on the phone and needs to know where to take Peter's body."

"What are you talking about?"

"The gentleman on the phone wants to know where you want Peter's body to be taken. Where will he be buried?"

"He needs to be at Fern Hill. That's where his cousin Jason is. He needs to be with Jason." I'm feeling panic at this question, and I hear my voice rise. "Why isn't he there? Where's he now?" Dad says that because the accident was in the neighboring county, they had to take him to the closest mortuary there.

My tone turns demanding. "Well, they need to move him, but I need to see him first. I need to go there and see him now, but the kids can't go. Tell them I'm coming to see him."

Dad continues talking on the phone and I hear him say, "Okay. We'll wait to hear back." Then he hangs up.

"Wait for what?!"

He explains they aren't sure I can go see him today, but are contacting the mortuary to find out.

"No. I'll see him today. They'll let me come see him! You call them and tell them I'm on my way. I'll see him today!" My dad gets back on the phone, and I hear him insisting and pleading on my behalf. When he hangs up, he says we can go, but it must be soon because they won't wait for us.

I ask my mom to stay with the kids because Patty and Daryl are on their way to meet us here and my dad is driving us to the mortuary where Peter is. Wait, it's just his body. He's not there. But maybe if we get there and I touch him, he'll wake up. Maybe he just needs me to be next to him and feel me and then he'll come back to me. Like Sleeping Beauty, right? Can that happen? *Please, God, make that happen.*

Daryl climbs into the front seat of the car with my dad while Patty and I sit in the back.

The mortuary is in Raymond and the drive there feels like the longest drive of my life. As we pass the place where Peter died, I slide my hand over and quietly hold Patty's as I keep my eyes focused on the passing scene. Everything was cleaned up and the only sign of the accident remaining was a broken fence and some small debris on the ground. His truck was gone. Already been taken to the tow yard. I was so thankful for the family who drove to the lot to retrieve his belongings. He had a lot of hunting and fishing gear with him. I know that was a great task and one done out of love. I'm so thankful for them.

We drive past the cranberry bogs and, still holding Patty's hand, I watch as the road winds over the rivers that feed out to the bay. I just keep praying that we'll get there and it will all be just a bad dream. He's going to be okay. He'll take a breath and wake up. He just has to. I can't do this without him.

We arrive at the mortuary just before their closing time and are greeted by a not-so-pleasant owner who is visibly annoyed about our arrival. I don't care what he thinks or feels at this moment. I just follow his lead to where Peter is lying. He motions to a small viewing room draped with red velvet curtains and steps aside, allowing me to proceed. I step forward and lift my left hand behind me motioning everyone else to stay back and let me go in by myself. I hold my breath as I move forward and whisper, "Please, God. Please."

The curtain is pulled back just enough to allow me to move through without touching it, and I see him lying there motionless. He's so still. He looks like he's simply taking a nap. There are no visible marks on him. No signs of someone who's been in an accident. As I move closer to him,

Don't Worry—I Have a Plan.

I see pieces of broken glass in his hair. I'm afraid to touch him, but force myself to clean the glass away. As I'm removing the last piece, I lean forward to kiss him on the forehead. He's so cold. I watch his chest, begging for movement. Searching for some signs of life, but don't see anything. He's gone and this is just his body. He isn't here and the reality of this is overwhelming. I take a final moment and then excuse myself to another room and allow Patty and Daryl to see him.

It's mere moments later that we're asked to leave so they can close. They explain that they've made arrangements for him to be moved to Fern Hill so he can be prepared and buried near family. It occurs to me that funeral and burial arrangements need to be made. This is good. I can turn my focus to the plans for his funeral and burial.

The ride home is mostly quiet, and I'm grateful for the silence so I can just watch the scenery and try to think about what needs to be done next. I'm unsure of what the next steps are, though, because I haven't been through this before. I realize there's a conversation happening in the car, but it sounds distant. I can feel the tears and realize they haven't stopped all day. I wonder if they ever will. Surely, I'll dry up and the tears will stop at some point. We're passing back by the place where his truck rolled and he died. I feel a hand grab mine, and I'm convinced the tears will never stop.

—◄o►—

As we come up to the house, I see many cars and can feel my heart pounding in my chest at the thought of facing everyone. At least for the moment my heart still works, and I wonder how much longer it will continue to beat. After the car is parked, I just sit, not wanting to go inside and find who may be there. But then I think of the kids—I need to know where they are and whom they're talking to. I find them inside the house with my mom and countless other people.

All these faces looking at me and searching my face for answers I don't have. *He's dead, people. That's the story. Thank you for being here, but I don't know what you could possibly do for me and the kids because you can't bring him back, and sitting here being sad isn't helpful.* I don't say a word though. Instead, I find the kids and hug them.

Sarah starts melting down, and I try to console her with no success. I can feel her sadness turning to anger, so I take her to the one place where we can be alone—the bathroom. I sit on the floor with her and rock her as she gets her emotions out and just cry with her. It's all I know to do. I let her scream for as long as she needs, until she's unable to cry any longer and I hold her exhausted little body in my arms.

After a few quiet moments, Sarah remembers there are people in the house she wants to see, so we leave the bathroom and rejoin the throng. Somehow it's early evening, and I find myself feeling grateful for those who are making sure my kids are eating and for taking them to play outside, distracting them from all the sadness inside.

I feel someone grab my arm and gently lead me to a chair at the dining room table. They put a plate of food in front of me: "You haven't eaten at all today. Here are a few options. Try to eat something." There's no way I can eat. The thought of food is repulsive. I just let the plate sit there. I look up and see my lifelong best friend, Julie. She hugs me and says she's here for me and the kids and will be staying at her mom and dad's for as long as I need. I find comfort in this, knowing she'll be nearby and ready at the first ring of her phone to do anything I need. I can't seem to reply with anything more than a nod.

I hear the door open again and don't even want to look at who may be there, but do anyway, and my friends Andrea and Malynnda are walking in. Malynnda grew up with Peter and was dear to him. He always spoke fondly of her. Andrea was with me from the beginning of my and Peter's relationship, and here she was now at the end. She has always been my no b.s. friend. She can look at my face and read my mood better than anyone, and I see by the look on her face and her purposeful stride she's here to do just that. She zeroes in on me, putting a hand up to stop those trying to greet her. She grabs me by my shoulders and looks me square in the eyes.

"Yep," she says, nodding her head with tears rolling down her cheeks. "I just needed to see your face."

The sobs are caught in my throat, and with a shrug and smug tone I choke out, "Well, here it is."

Don't Worry—I Have a Plan.

Tears streaming down our faces, she grabs and pulls me into a strong, unbreakable embrace. She holds me for a moment, looks at my face again, and then turns and glances over her shoulder at Malynnda, who is standing behind her with a river of tears quietly flowing down her cheeks. Her eyes tell me everything she wants to say but can't. Andrea looks back at me, nodding her head.

"Okay," she says. Then almost as quickly as she arrived, she leaves. Surprisingly that moment, that embrace, gives me the strength to take care of the next set of details.

"I want the service to be on Saturday," I say to whoever is listening. The quiet conversations around me cease. "I need it to be on Saturday. I can't wait a week or longer, and I want Reverend Hopely to do the service. He's the one who helped bring Peter back to church and made the connection of God's love for him. He needs to do the service." I don't even know who I'm talking to at this moment, but hear people scrambling and phone calls being made.

"Also, does anyone know where Mike Flanagan is? Does he know what's happened and can he get home for the service? He needs to be here. I need him to be here." Mike was Peter's childhood friend who'd been closer to him than a brother. Their connection ran deep, and Peter always said that no amount of time or distance between them could break their bond.

I feel the need to get things organized but also feel the overwhelming desire to slip through the door to my right, crawl into bed, and slowly fade into nothingness. As I contemplate which choice to make, I turn toward the windows looking out over the yard where my babies are playing and, at that moment, make the choice to continue.

Today, I'll stay.

For them.

◄◌►

I need to get away from the people and the noise, so I walk to the back of the house and stand looking out the back windows toward the bay, trying to find some peace. I feel the heaviness of the loss and the overwhelming feeling of loneliness. I've lost my best friend, and this loneliness is my life now. As I try to drown out the noise around me, I can hear my mom from afar saying someone is here to see me, but I ignore her. There have been a hundred people here today, and I can't bring myself to turn around and see whom she's talking about. I hear her tell whoever it is that I'm in the back. I don't move. I can't move. I'm frozen in this spot, and this is where I may stay for the rest of my life. A fixed figure for people to gaze at, standing between the washing machine and freezer. The hillside and bay in the distance my view forevermore.

I feel arms wrap around me, bringing me back to the reality of the moment, and hear a broken voice whisper in my ear, "Oh, Steph, I'm so sorry." It's Mark Tucker, Peter's best friend. I crumble as he hugs me and just holds me as I weep. When I'm able to speak, I beg him for the answer to the biggest question hanging over me.

"What am I supposed to do?"

"I don't know, Steph, but Holly and I are here for you and the kids." All I can do is let him hug me while I collapse into a pile of tears.

CHAPTER 10

The Tree That Stands Alone

I was unsure how it had happened, but the sun had set, which meant it was past the kids' bedtime. All visitors other than my parents and Julie had left, and I was using every bit of strength to get my babies ready for bed. They wanted to sleep with me in my bed, and I was more than happy to oblige. I wanted them as near to me as possible, and although their bedrooms were just upstairs, it felt as though they were on the other side of the world. As I got us ready for bed, my mom let me know she'd be staying on the sofa in case I needed anything.

"Thanks, Mom, but I think we'll be okay," I said.

"Nevertheless, I'll be just out here if you need something."

I hugged her and went about the bedtime routine, feeling thankful for the routine I didn't need to put any thought into. The kids and I crawled into bed and snuggled up tight until they fell asleep.

I know I fell asleep for a while, but woke up in the middle of the night gasping for air. I couldn't breathe and felt panicked. I tried to gain control so I wouldn't wake the kids sleeping soundly next to me. As I woke up fully, the reality of what had happened came flooding back into my mind. I sat rocking back and forth on the side of the bed, quietly sobbing. I was trying hard to fall apart quietly so I didn't wake the kids, but wasn't so quiet that my mom couldn't hear me. I imagine she never went to sleep just in case she was needed. She rushed in like she did when I was a kid having a nightmare, wrapped her arms around me and just held me while I cried.

My mom is a doer. A fixer. If you need a button sewn on or a hem fixed, she's on it. If you need laundry washed, cleaning, or organizing done, she's your gal. She'll pull appliances out to scrub the baseboards behind them, and will take care of your dogs, chickens, and horses too. If she feels there's a need she can meet or a task she can complete, she won't sit by idly. It brings her joy to help others. I know at that moment, though, she felt helpless. As a mom myself, I can't imagine how much it broke her heart to see me going through that much pain and heartache, knowing there was nothing she could do to make it better. There were not enough cleaning products to wash away the hurt or enough needle and thread to mend my shattered heart. All she could do was sit with me and watch me hurt, and I know that destroyed her.

After what felt like hours of sitting on the edge of my bed crying, I was able to communicate what I needed. I needed to go through pictures. I needed to pick some out for the service, and I needed to see his face. My mom had direction and went to work getting my picture boxes out of the attic. Peter's cousin had volunteered to do a video for the service, and I needed to make sure he had the pictures I wanted of Peter and the kids. My friend and Peter's pseudo-sister Tina had called and reminded me of the song he'd always wanted played at his service. I was thankful to have one less thing to think about and grateful she'd remembered details like that.

One of the first pictures we came across was of Peter and the elk he got during the last hunting season. It was the one he snuck Perry out of church to retrieve from the woods. It was a great picture of him with the biggest smile and happiness in his eyes. *This is the one people will want to see*, I thought. *This is Peter.*

My heart ached as we continued looking through the pictures and setting aside the ones that held the most cherished memories for me and the kids. Lining them up on the dining room table allowed me to see our entire married life. It was a bittersweet moment of thankfulness for what we had but also absolute heartache for what the kids and I had just lost. Our best friend was gone, and there would be no new memories to cherish with him.

◄o►

I was able to go back to bed before Perry and Sarah woke up, and when I could see dawn peeking through the bedroom window, all I wanted to do was stay in bed with my kids. I didn't want to get up and talk to anyone or deal with anything. I wanted to keep them safe in my arms and protect them from everything happening around us. To my dismay, that wasn't an option, because I'd insisted on having Peter's service on the Saturday. It was Thursday, so that meant we had a lot of planning and decision-making to get everything pulled together in two days. I didn't know what decisions I'd even need to make, but was determined to make sure the important things—his obituary, what music would be played, and what words would be spoken about him at his funeral—would get done.

As I made my way to the kitchen for a cup of coffee I didn't end up drinking, I looked around at my dining room and living room in amazement at the scene in front of me. In a single day my house had become a flower shop, overflowing with the most beautiful plants and arrangements. So many people had sent flowers and cards. I was overwhelmed by the outpouring of love and affection from my community and stood there taking in the sight. Weeping, I wished I could go back in time, send them all back, and undo what had happened the day before.

In the midst of all of it, I was able to untangle my thoughts and take a moment to look at each floral arrangement and plant, reading the cards attached. The kids and I were surrounded by an ocean of love from our people.

It was still early morning when my front door opened and people poured in. When my dad arrived, he pulled me aside to talk about how many people were coming to the house. He was worried that, with the trauma the kids and I had experienced along with the lack of sleep, I was one hug away from getting sick. He'd also observed that people were showing up distraught and inconsolable and although they intended to be a support to me, it was me who ended up comforting and consoling them. I wasn't getting renewed with support but was getting sucked dry of every ounce of energy left in my body.

"Stephanie, I'm concerned. You're going to get sick and don't have the strength to deal with that right now."

"I'll be fine," I said, waving my hand in the air. "I can't turn people away. They're here to help me."

He asked me to at least sit down and eat something. I reluctantly agreed to sit at the table, and someone brought a plate and set it in front of me. I stared at the slices of bell peppers and carrots, cheese, and crackers with a dollop of ranch dip. The thought of putting any food in my mouth still made me sick to my stomach. I pushed some things around on the plate and dipped some veggies in the ranch hoping to make it look like I'd eaten, then put it aside and walked away.

Today was the day we were meeting at Fern Hill to discuss burial arrangements, so I'd have to leave the house and be gone for several hours, and was okay with that. I didn't want to admit that my dad was right, but I did need a break from comforting others, even if it meant having to take care of these details. I was feeling very task-oriented, so having decisions to make was helpful for me to keep moving forward.

I needed to pick out some clothes for Peter to be buried in. I knew he'd prefer to be buried in sweats and a hoodie. He'd most likely prefer the hoodie with the sleeves cut off and the front pocket missing, but that wasn't going to happen.

Peter, you got your way with almost everything, and if you'd told me ahead of time what you wanted to be buried in, I might have given you that. But you didn't, so it was my choice, and you were dressed nicely. No sweatpants and no hoodie. You can take that up with me later.

My dad was again our chauffeur and took me with Patty and Daryl to the funeral home. Before we left, I gave my mom and Julie strict instructions to not take their eyes off my babies. "Do *not* let anyone take them anywhere or sit and cry all over them. Promise me." Julie nodded and my mom hugged me and patted my hands, assuring me she wouldn't let them out of her sight.

Don't Worry—I Have a Plan.

━◦►

I didn't know what to expect at the funeral home. I'd never been through this process before, nor had I talked to anybody who had. The kind, welcoming director led us to a small room with a conference table lined with chairs. As we sat down, I scanned the room and realized we were surrounded by a variety of wood grains, silk and satin fabric swatches, and brass and silver hardware as well as a surprisingly large variety of urns. I couldn't get my brain to process all my eyes were seeing. It was just too much to take in.

The director was compassionate and thorough in explaining what needed to be done and what we could choose to do. They couldn't prepare Peter's body in time to do the burial on the same day as his service, and I found myself feeling relieved hearing that. I didn't want the whole town at his graveside. I needed it to be just family and a few close friends.

I told them I wanted him buried as close to his cousin Jason as possible, and they were able to find a plot in the same section and only a couple of rows away. It was perfect and I was thankful. After confirming his plot, the director looked at me and started to talk about his casket. As those words reached my ears, I crumbled, burying my face in my hands and crying. "I can't make this decision! I just can't!"

Patty shot across the table, grabbing for me. "Don't worry, baby, we'll do it. We'll pick out the best for our boy."

I couldn't move. All the shock and disbelief I'd been working to keep at bay consumed me. As they left the room with the director to choose Peter's casket, I collapsed against my dad, and he held me as we let the grief run through us.

When we were able to gather ourselves together, we went to the foyer to wait. Patty and Daryl returned, and Patty told me in detail what they'd chosen, but I honestly couldn't comprehend, nor do I remember anything she said. I knew it would be beautiful, and I was grateful they were able to make some of those decisions for and with me.

I only made it halfway to the car before I remembered something and ran back to the foyer. I was just able to catch the director.

"Is there something else I can help you with?" he asked.

"I need his wedding ring," I said. "Can I please have his ring?"

He kindly explained he'd do his best but that sometimes it was difficult to remove rings. My stomach lurched and he disappeared down the hallway. *Oh, God, please let them be able to get his ring*, I silently begged while I waited for him to return. I'd not expected to hear those words at all and wasn't prepared to deal with the disappointment of not getting his ring. That ring, while a simple gold band, was a symbol of our lifelong commitment to each other, and while that bond had been broken by his death, I had an indescribable need to have and hold it.

The director returned and gently handed the ring to me. Afraid I'd drop it, I slid it onto my thumb and carefully folded my thumb over into my palm, wrapping my other fingers around to protect it from falling to the ground. I weakly whispered a thank you and slipped out the door.

On the drive home we discussed plans for the service, what we all wanted and needed, and how we'd pull it all together in two short days. Short days? Each one of those days felt like a lifetime. Every minute felt like a month and every hour a year. Time was all but standing still as I worked to concentrate on just taking the next breath.

I recalled hearing people talk about the pain of losing the one you love and thinking how horrible it must all be, but this was a pain impossible to explain with words. Our human vocabulary doesn't carry any description strong enough for our brains or hearts to understand. If you're thinking you can imagine how difficult it is, think of the pain you're imagining and multiply it by about a million and one. Then you may be close.

When we pulled up to my house, I saw a lawn mower disappear around the back side of the house. It looked like someone was mowing my yard, but I couldn't figure out what was going on because the lawn mower I saw wasn't my lawn mower. I saw the mower come back around the corner and recognized one of our lifelong family friends doing the mowing. I didn't know what to think. I took a lot of pride in taking care of my home, and mowing the grass was something I always did. I hadn't had time to mow in the last week, though, and the spring rain had made the grass grow quickly. A feeling of failure washed over me, followed quickly by overwhelming gratitude for our friend. He'd lost his wife several years prior, and now was taking care of my yard after I'd just lost my husband.

I looked at my dad. "Why is he doing this? He doesn't need to."

"Yes, he does. Let him do this for you," Dad said. I didn't have the energy to argue, and something in my heart understood what was happening at that moment.

Sixteen years later, I know that healing was happening. When I can reach out to someone who has lost their spouse and offer any kind of comfort, it provides a little piece of healing for me. I'm grateful for the other person who allows me to show them love and understanding in any form. I thought this man was giving me a gift but, in a way, I think maybe he was receiving a gift as well.

◄○►

So many people continued to come and go throughout the day. Julie was there every day with gifts and hot cocoa for my kids. Giving is her love language and she's amazing at it. She poured love over my kids and me and was ready to jump in and help with any detail needed. It was such a blessing to have her at the house. When I was feeling overwhelmed with visitors, I was able to just look at her and she'd masterfully step in and help guide them in another direction. She appeared out of nowhere regularly to pick something up, run an errand, and tend to the kids and their needs during a time when each thought was interrupted by a reminder of what we'd just lost.

Julie was probably thankful when my dad made the announcement Friday that he was locking my front door and hanging a sign telling people I was taking a break from visitors. This gave her time to leave for a bit and rest. Dad was still worried about my health, and even though I felt obligated to welcome all who showed up, I also knew I needed a break.

I couldn't stay in the house and watch people arrive just to be turned away, so decided to take the kids to the nearby hotel where Patty's family was staying. The kids could play with their cousins in the pool, and I could visit with the family. I decided this would be a good thing.

We were only there for a little while before I found it extremely difficult to follow the conversations. Peter's cousins were talking about the video that his cousin Jerry was putting together and how much time that was taking him. "He's staying up all night to get it done," one of them said. One cousin was busying herself with a mirror and tweezers, taking care to pluck her eyebrows just right and explaining all the different tweezer types she'd tried over the years and which were her favorite. I felt like the family was trying to do small talk for my benefit, but couldn't seem to engage with more than a nod or an "Uh-huh."

They were all so full of life even in the darkest time, and while most days I'd find their energy comforting and uplifting, my head was spinning. *Hold it together*, I told myself. *The kids need this time away from the house.* But the more I tried to track the rapid-fire conversation, the more panicked I felt. I was screaming inside with the chatter and laughter happening around me and wanted to crawl out of my skin and run from the building.

The conversation turned to Patty and Daryl and how they were not handling the loss well. *Of course, they aren't! They've just lost their only son! Their world is falling apart around them!*

They kept circling back to Patty and how she wouldn't get off her lawn mower or talk to anybody. They were trying to decide what they were going to do to get her off the lawn mower. I thought I was only thinking my response in my head, but then heard myself talking out loud and realized everyone else had stopped talking.

"You'll do nothing. You'll leave her alone. She's on her lawn mower because it's the only place she can be alone. The lawn mower keeps people away. As long as she's on it, nobody can touch her—she's safe."

The looks that I perceived as not understanding were probably more of surprise that I'd opened my mouth and spoken. "She's processing," I told them. "She'll get off the lawn mower when she's ready. Leave her alone until then." After a short pause, the chatter resumed, and I wondered if I really had spoken out loud.

I knew the kids were enjoying themselves, but I had to leave. I thanked everyone for allowing us to escape for a bit, gathered Perry and Sarah, and went home. I'd hoped to find some relief in being out of the house, but left the hotel feeling more exhausted and overwhelmed.

Upon returning home, I unlocked the front door and tore the sign off the glass inset. If people wanted to come and see me, they could. There was no telling what they were going to get, if they got anything at all, but were welcome to show up. And they did. They brought cards, food, flowers, and gifts for the kids, and I continued to feel overwhelmed by the outpouring of love. My refrigerator and freezers were full, and my house was overflowing with plants and flowers.

Two of the last visitors that day were Andrea's parents, Marshall and Teresa. They were as close to me as family, had been my youth pastors during high school, and had been there from the moment Peter and I had started dating. They knew and loved me, and I loved and respected them. They asked me to walk them out to their car and away from the people in the house. Teresa walked me to the middle of my front yard. She grabbed both of my hands and, with great intensity, looked me directly in the eyes: "Listen to what I'm about to say to you."

I glanced at Marshall, the "gentle giant" as I referred to him, and he gave me the raised eyebrows "You better listen" look. So, I returned my attention to Teresa. She squeezed my hands in hers as her eyes bore into my soul. She waved one hand toward the trees lining my property.

"Stephanie, look at those trees. See how they stand together?" I looked over at the trees and nodded my head. "Now, look at me." I looked back at her as she continued to look at me intently. "A tree that stands alone will surely fall in the storm, but the tree that stands in a group will draw strength and protection from those around it, being able to withstand the storm."

I felt puzzled by her words. I was exhausted and at the time quite honestly thought, *Okay, whatever. Thank you for your wise words, oh ancient one, but I have to go now and deal with my reality.* Instead, I looked at her and nodded. "Thank you. I know." Even though I didn't. I hugged each of them and took my time walking back to the house.

Several days later when I had some time to reflect on her words, I realized that she did speak with wisdom, and I knew she was right. I couldn't travel this road by myself. I had God with me, but I also needed people to help. But who?

The answer came in a special delivery the week following the funeral, but I had no idea at the time how incredible the gift was God was giving me. Sitting on my front step was a coffee-mug-shaped pot with flowers in it. The card attached simply read, "We meet for coffee every morning. Join us when you're ready." It was signed by Andrea and Malynnda. I was deeply moved by this kind gesture and thought maybe I could join them at some point—I knew they'd welcome me with open arms and there would be no judgment or advice. But I wasn't sure I was ready to have "coffee talk" with anyone yet.

CHAPTER 11

The White Cross

I was thankful to hear my dad had connected with Reverend Hopely, who agreed to help with Peter's service. If we had Reverend Hopely and Pastor Ness, our current pastor, leading the service and Jerry putting together the slideshow, I was okay with any of the other details that needed to be ironed out. Patty and Daryl had some requests, and I wanted to make sure their needs were met. But most of all I wanted to make sure that through the words spoken at the service our kids heard that their dad loved them and he loved Jesus.

Peter wasn't raised in church, and his actions weren't always what you would call traditional Christian behavior, so it would be understandable if someone who didn't know him closely didn't know he believed in God. I was recently given a gift by way of a conversation with a new friend. Her husband, whom Peter always spoke highly of, was acquainted with Peter through commercial fishing. My new friend had never met Peter, but her husband relayed stories of him and their interactions, and even though they never spoke of God directly, he told her that he felt Peter was a believer. Knowing that others saw this in him was precious to me: just recalling that conversation brings tears to my eyes.

Having Peter attend church with me while we were dating was a treat. I knew it wasn't his favorite thing to do and knew a lot of his motivation was his desire to date me, and I was okay with that. We always sat in the back with friends and Peter's inability to sit still created distractions to those around him, me included. This bothered some of the adults. So, one Sunday one of the men in church took it upon himself to interrupt the pastor to address the kids in the back. Most specifically, he addressed Peter for being disruptive. His approach to address the issue felt like an attempt to publicly shame and embarrass us.

After that finger-wagging speech, pointing Peter out for "being disruptive," Peter stormed out in a cloud of middle fingers and didn't return. Were we being disruptive? We most certainly were. Was it appropriate for someone to address our behavior? Absolutely. Was it necessary that we be addressed publicly in front of the entire congregation? Definitely not.

We were in the wrong, but instead of having grace and love extended, we were shamed and embarrassed. In that single moment, Peter was made to feel he wasn't welcome because he didn't "behave" the way others expected him to. That moment shaped how he viewed church for years to come.

I continued to attend regularly, and he never spoke against my going, but didn't feel welcome anymore. I understood where he was coming from and wanted him to attend with me, but didn't push. I just kept praying and inviting.

Before we got married, we had some premarital meetings with Reverend Hopely, the pastor at my church at that time. He was welcoming and nonjudgmental and made Peter feel at ease. When Peter swore in front of him, I cringed, but Reverend Hopely didn't even blink an eye. For once, Peter didn't feel shamed by a Christian for being who he was. He didn't feel unwelcome because he didn't act or talk in a way considered acceptable. Reverend Hopely accepted him as he was—just as Jesus would do. I believe that moment was the beginning of a change in Peter and our relationship. He still didn't come to church with me regularly, but happily accepted invitations to have dinner with the Reverend and his family, and had enormous respect for him. I believe it was because he experienced the grace of God through him.

Reverend Hopely ended up moving out of state and I changed churches. In the year before Peter's death, I connected with a small Bible study group that he eventually started attending with me. It was nothing short of miraculous to not just have him with me but to have him engaged in the study. He asked questions, challenged beliefs, and left every week feeling he'd learned something new about the Bible and God. I watched him grow in his walk with the Lord and was thankful. I wanted this reflected in the words spoken about him at his service. He loved the Lord and he loved people, and his family needed to hear this.

I didn't know what to expect from the funeral at the church. I'd only attended a few funerals in my lifetime, and the most recent had been my grandfather's just a year prior. I hadn't fully healed from that loss, and thoughts of him and his service ran through my head as we planned Peter's. My grandfather was one of my favorite people, and we were very close. Losing him was the most difficult experience I'd ever endured up to this moment. As I reflected on the pain I'd felt during his service, I wondered how I'd possibly be able to make it through Peter's.

I don't remember how all the details came together, but know that I had an amazing church and family who simply made it happen. Leading up to the service, my dear friend Tina called a few times: "Stephanie, the church isn't big enough. You need to have his service at the high school."

I knew the high school would be more accommodating, but my mind wasn't thinking about accommodating the large group of people who would be in attendance. "No, I'm not having it at the high school. It will be at the church and I'm not changing my mind." I was thinking only of my children. I knew they could be going to that high school someday, and I wouldn't let this be their memory every time they walked into that gymnasium. I wouldn't do that to them. There might be standing room only in the church, but his service wasn't going to be at the school.

As we all sat at my dining table and continued plans for the service, there was an interruption: "Stephanie, somebody put a white cross up on the side of the highway where Peter died."

My stomach dropped and I felt instant rage as I heard this. *Are you kidding me? Who would have done that? Nobody talked to me or asked me what I thought about this.* They were explaining that someone went to the high school and asked students in the woodshop class to make a cross, paint it white, and then this person posted it on the side of the highway where his truck went off the road. I felt sick and the room started spinning around me.

"No," I heard myself say. "Absolutely not. Take it out of the ground right now." The reaction on the faces around me told me my tone wasn't as calm as I thought it was, and they didn't agree with my reaction, but I was adamant. "Nobody talked to me and asked how I felt about this. I won't have a marker to scream out at our kids, 'This is where your dad died!' every time they pass that spot on the road. This isn't okay with me and how dare they do this without asking me first?" I realized at that point how venomously I was speaking, but also didn't care. We live in a small town and have a tight family, but when it came to Peter and the kids, I called the shots. Nobody else.

I'd always preferred for Peter to make most of the decisions for us. I didn't always agree and sometimes that led to intense discussion but, ultimately, we had the same goals and he seemed to be able to take a less emotional approach to things than I did. I also tended to put my needs aside to make others happy or keep the peace, unless it was something I felt really passionate about.

But now, two days after Peter's death, the instinct to lead our family was kicking in strongly. My first priorities were protecting my children and carrying on with what I knew Peter would have wanted, and there wasn't a soul alive who could have stopped me.

"It comes out today," I said.

There were murmurs of "Okay," "You got it," and "It will come out today" from around the room as people started to scatter.

"I want confirmation when it has been removed, please."

I don't want to be disrespectful to anyone who has a cross marking a spot for their loved one. I know this is a common practice and the intention behind this was that of kindness, but I didn't want a visual reminder for me or our family and friends whenever we drove the highway. We knew where the accident happened. To this day I can't pass that spot without seeing his truck up on end in the darkness with flashing emergency lights all around. I can't drive past the little store across the street without seeing the faces of those gathered in the parking lot watching me as I arrived to receive the devastating news that my husband had died. A white cross to signify what? That someone died there? Isn't there enough sadness in our lives without a visual reminder of a tragic death in our faces when all we want is to get from point A to point B? If point B is a happy destination, that white cross just put a wet blanket on the purpose of our journey.

It took less than an hour to receive confirmation that the cross had been removed, and I thought at that moment I'd been either very frightening in the delivery of my opinion, or had some of the most amazing people in my life who truly wanted to do what they could for me. I chose and continue to believe the latter.

CHAPTER 12

Eight Minutes and Fifty-Seven Seconds

The funeral felt so final—like it would be the closing chapter of my life with Peter—and I was finding it difficult to complete the simplest tasks. Even just the act of brushing my teeth felt monumental. I tried hard to concentrate on taking care of each task as it arose. I needed to get the kids' clothes ready. Since Easter had been the weekend before, thankfully they could wear their Easter clothes. My mom had washed and ironed them so they'd be perfect. How was it possible that a week prior we were a whole and happy family and suddenly, we were the remnants of that picture now shattered?

I needed to decide what I was going to wear. *Maybe if I don't find something appropriate, I won't have to go. Then we won't have the funeral and we can find a way to avoid it altogether.* I spent an unnecessary amount of time negotiating this option with myself until my rational side won. I decided to wear black slacks, a short-sleeved kelly-green blouse, and my black heels and take my black cardigan in case it was cold in the church.

As I dressed, I wondered how my clothes could fit so loosely after just a few days. My slacks hung on my hips, and as I put on my blouse, I felt like a little girl trying on her mom's clothes. I felt like a shrinking frame within the oversized fabric encompassing me. I know traditionally the widow would wear all black, but couldn't acknowledge myself as a widow yet. I couldn't even say the word *widow* in my head, let alone give myself that title. I didn't need to be in all black, so the kelly-green top was my silent protest to being a widow in mourning.

The kids and I loaded into my parents' car and rode to the church, where we'd face family, friends, and community members to publicly acknowledge the passing of my husband. I sat in the middle of the back seat and held my babies' hands as we made our way. We were escorted to a room behind the sanctuary where we'd wait with immediate family until the service started. This was done to protect us from being caught up in the crowd and being overwhelmed by people wanting to talk to us beforehand. I was extremely thankful for the person who was so thoughtful in this planning.

While we waited to be brought out, I thought of how I could enter the sanctuary so I'd look at as few people as possible. Perry was ready to join the party and Sarah was prepared to join his one-man parade. I knelt in front of them, held their hands, and quietly explained, "You two will stay with me. We'll go in as a family. The three of us will stick together because we're the family now."

An usher came into the room announcing it was time, and I had a brief flashback to the day of our wedding when I was escorted to the entrance of the sanctuary to meet my groom. The happiness of that day and the excitement I'd felt wanting to burst through the doors ready for everyone to see me make that lifelong commitment to Peter, to now, nine years later, standing at the door to his funeral, saying goodbye to the one I loved. This moment, such a stark contrast to our beautiful, joyous wedding day.

When we reached the sanctuary doors, I made a quick move and picked up Sarah. I held her on my left hip and grabbed Perry's hand with my right hand. It was a calculated move—I knew because we were entering from the right side of the sanctuary that if I held Sarah on my left hip, she'd be facing away from the crowd and she and her dress would hide me from a lot of the prying eyes. Keeping Perry on my right meant I could shield him from as many people as possible. This felt like the safest way to enter the large space where every inch was filled with grief.

Eight Minutes and Fifty-Seven Seconds

We walked in and my knees went weak. *Keep it together, just keep it together. Don't trip and don't pass out. Just walk to your seat and sit down. Be thankful you're in the front row and everyone will be behind you.*

I took a quick peek around. *Oh my goodness—there are so many people and so many flowers.* I felt the tears stinging my eyes and knew I had no control over them.

As we found our way to the seats designated for us at the front of the sanctuary, I did a quick scan of the area closest to me and locked eyes with Peter's Aunt Tammi. She was sitting with Uncle Arvid and others I couldn't bring my eyes to focus on because I couldn't break my focus away from her. I felt this sudden urge to run and just fall into her, but felt another strong resistance, knowing if I allowed her to touch me, I'd break. Her ability to love so fiercely would be the safe space I desired, but it would also render me incapable of tapping into the little bit of strength I had left, and I needed every ounce of that strength to make it through the day. I broke eye contact with her and, with as much grace and dignity as I could muster, took the seat that had been set aside for me.

I kept Sarah on my lap. I couldn't let go of her. I had this uncontrollable need to keep her as physically close to me as I could. As my gaze moved from my daughter's beautiful red hair to the floral arrangements so beautifully displayed directly in front of me, I saw an enormous, breathtaking arrangement from Kemper Sports. I squinted my eyes to see the card pinned to the large ribbon so perfectly tied to the vase, and could make out the message of condolence on the front. Tears began to flow down my face. I'd lost all control over the tears that decided to come and go on their own without any regard for me or my surroundings. I kept my attention fixed on the amazing arrangement gifted by a company that had only partnered with our company a short time ago. While the words on the card were generic words of condolence, I was deeply moved by their generosity. I decided that arrangement, those words, would be the perfect focal point for me throughout the service. If I studied those flowers so beautifully situated in front of me, I didn't have to focus on anything else.

My plan worked well until the video started playing, and then I couldn't peel my eyes away from the pictures projected onto the large screen at the front of the sanctuary. The presentation of Peter's life was beautifully created for everyone in attendance. Pictures from his birth to childhood and high school years, to our wedding and our precious family so carefully choreographed in time to his favorite song, "Dream On," by Aerosmith, and the song we danced our first dance to, "Faithfully" by Journey. How does someone's entire life fit into the length of two songs? Watching each picture flash for a moment caused my broken heart to work harder to keep beating, and I found myself wishing I could jump up, grab him off the screen, and pull him back into my life. I wondered how his parents could sit and watch the life of their son begin and end in the span of two songs.

Eight minutes and fifty-seven seconds was the time it took to portray his thirty-three years, two months, and twenty-seven days of life. How is that fair?

I was thankful for Reverend Hopely and Pastor Ness who, together, took those eight minutes and fifty-seven seconds and expanded them with their words to appropriately honor Peter's life. They were able to talk frankly about who he was as a person, husband, father, and friend. These two men, who knew Peter during different times of his life, were able to talk about his walk with faith. They acknowledged his struggle with religion and attending church but expressed how that didn't deter his belief in God or his desire to support his family to walk in faith. Reverend Hopely and Pastor Ness, with the help of many of our friends and family, did an exquisite job honoring my husband.

I knew a host of people had attended Peter's service, but didn't realize just how many until a month or so later. I was at the bank and the teller helping me with my transaction leaned toward me and quietly said, "My son drove past the church on the day of your husband's service, and said he wished he'd known him. He figured he must have been a really great guy. I asked him why he said that, and he replied that only someone really special would have that many people at their funeral." I didn't understand. Of course, Peter was special, but most funerals in our town were well attended. I looked at her, confused, and asked, "What do you mean 'that many people'? There was standing room only, but that's because I chose a smaller venue."

"Stephanie, there were cars parked close to a mile down the highway in both directions from the church." I was stunned and know my face told her everything I was thinking. A hushed and vulnerable "Oh" was the only response I could offer. I thanked her quickly for helping me and for sharing the story of her son and quickly fled to my car.

A month after the funeral and I was just realizing the number of people who'd shown up! Those who'd been impacted by Peter or his family or mine. I was overwhelmed with emotion at the thought of the multitude who cared. The love of my community kept showing up in the most beautiful ways.

◄○►

After the service, everyone proceeded to the community recreation hall near our house to eat and visit and share stories about Peter. Some amazing women had gathered and made food to serve the masses. How they pulled this off in three days still astonishes me. However, it's the perfect example of the superpower my community possesses. They make things like a funeral reception in three days happen and do so graciously. As exhausted as I was to have the people around, I don't know what I'd have done without them. They each have served such a great purpose and need for me and my children and there's no way I'll be able to repay them. Ever.

The reception was packed. I stood in the middle of the room greeting one person after another. Glancing over to my left, I saw Uncle John and Aunt Linnea seated at a table with my parents. I exchanged a look with my uncle and as I tried to make my way over to them, kept getting stopped. Finally able to get to them, I got the hug I needed. I couldn't tell you what Uncle John said to me, but it brought great comfort. I was able to sit with them and visit briefly before being pulled away to talk to more people.

I could feel my energy being drained with each person I hugged and talked to in the long line of those waiting. Each desired to give me words of encouragement and condolence, which I appreciated, but it also left me feeling exhausted. I looked up from what felt like the one-hundredth person I'd hugged that afternoon and saw the face I'd been waiting for. He'd made it!

I saw him standing patiently with his hands folded casually in front of him and his face reflecting the grief I felt. Peter's childhood best friend Mike was there, and I couldn't say a word as I reached for him, and he just hugged me. His hugs could heal a thousand wounds, which made the tears flow freely because the comfort I felt at that moment allowed me to just breathe. He quietly asked if he could see the kids and, since I couldn't get any words out, I just nodded, grabbed his hand, and led him outside, where they were playing.

"There's our little princess in the creamy white dress and sweater tied around her waist playing with no regard in the sand pile, and over there is our little man running around the grass field with his friends." I called them over and reintroduced them to Mike. They'd met him years before, but I knew they wouldn't remember him because they were so young. "Mike was your dad's best friend growing up. They were like brothers." Mike shared a few fun memories of growing up with their dad, and watching their faces as they listened melted me. They needed this moment to hear good stories and happy memories of their dad after a day of sadness and grief. I realized how much I needed it as well as I discovered I was smiling for the first time in days.

Peter's good friend Jamey joined Mike and me outside. We visited for a while and their mere presence brought me comfort. I felt a deep appreciation for the affection they showed for Peter and for me and my children. For the first time in the last three days, I felt safe and able to just breathe easily for a moment. As we stood together reminiscing, I saw one of our town's prominent businesswomen walking my way. With the assistance of her friend, she was making her way across the uneven grassy field. I excused myself and quickly walked toward her. She extended her condolences and handed me a card: "I wanted to make sure you got this directly from me."

I was deeply touched by her presence at the service. "Thank you so much, Neddie. You have no idea how much it means to me that you're here."

She nodded her understanding, looked me directly in the eyes, and grabbed my hand. "You take care of yourself," she said, with a seriousness that was more than just a nice thing to say. Neddie was one of the strongest women I'd ever known, and a recent widow herself. I had an immense amount of respect for her and was able to see there was a deeper meaning to the words she spoke. The unspoken piece of her message was reflected in her eyes, and I understood her completely.

I watched Neddie walk away and suddenly felt the emotion of the last four days settling on me. I just couldn't handle any more of this day. I didn't want to take the kids away while they were playing and they seemed to be doing well, so found someone to keep an eye on them and walked home.

I don't know how long everyone stayed at the reception, but I couldn't go back, and hoped that didn't offend anybody. I just needed quiet time at my home. All I was able to do was sit on the sofa and stare at Peter's coat hanging by the front door with his shoes on the floor beneath it. *He'll never walk through that door again and he'll never again wear that coat or those shoes.* I couldn't bear the thought of moving forward with life knowing he wouldn't be there with me.

CHAPTER 13

Remember
What I Promised

Sunday, April 23 ended up being a welcomed quiet day. I chose not to go to church and just stayed home to rest and take care of things around the house. I needed a day of recovery between the funeral and the burial. I didn't have the stamina to endure both of those events without being able to take a breath in between.

The sun was shining, and the crisp, clean smell of spring enveloped us. I wanted the kids to play outside for fun instead of being kept from the house for fear they'd hear too many details of funeral planning. So, we all spent time in the yard and my mom helped me with some gardening. I loved spending time in my garden. Peter had marked off a twenty-by-fifty-foot section of the yard, built a fence that didn't keep the dog out, added some raised beds, and tilled the rest so I could have a garden space to enjoy. I loved every second of planning, planting, and caring for my garden. Digging in the dirt was a form of therapy for me, and having my garden to work in that day was a gift.

We'd spent countless hours consulting our gardening neighbor on the appropriate time to plant and the right way to fertilize to make sure the soil pH was optimal for growing vegetables. He'd lean across the fence answering our questions as he repeatedly threw a stick or ball or what-ever was brought to him by our black lab, Onyx, or "Swamp Dog," as he called her. We got her when Perry was just a few months old, and she was the best dog we ever had. She'd often play with the neighborhood dogs in the swamp below our house, and every day when our neighbor came home from work, she'd run from the swamp to greet him and happily finish the leftovers in his lunch box.

In the afternoon, Peter's aunt who lived nearby came over to say hello and see how we were doing. We weren't particularly close, but were friendly with each other and checked in on each other occasionally. She extended her condolences and asked, "Is there anything you need? You or the kids?"

"Thank you. I think we're okay for right now, but appreciate your asking." I took a breath to steady myself before the next words came out. "Do you know the burial is tomorrow? I want to keep it to just family and close friends, so want to make sure you know about it."

"Yes, yes. We know and we'll be there." She looked toward Onyx sitting at my feet and pointed at her. "Looks like you've been able to get Onyx to calm down." With everything going on, I hadn't paid close attention to our dog, so wasn't sure what she was talking about.

"What do you mean?" I asked.

She told me she'd brought her treats the last few days. "She's been sitting at the edge of the driveway crying. I figured she was waiting for Peter but knew he wasn't coming home. Dogs sense these things, you know, and it made me sad for her."

With those words, the last little bit of my already broken heart crumbled. Of course. Onyx was Peter's dog, and had sensed his death. I looked down and Onyx looked up at me with eyes full of pain. She was doing what she could to be near me and comfort me. "Oh, you poor thing." I sat down, pulled her close, and hugged her as she nuzzled her head against my neck. Tears streamed down my face. Does grief know no bounds?

◄○►

A little while later my aunt Yvette stopped by as she was heading back home to Idaho. She visited with my mom and, when she was ready to leave, I walked down the front path with her. She hugged me for a long time, then told me of a woman in her church who'd lost her husband when her kids were young. "This woman has remarried, Stephanie. She said she'd be happy to meet with you and talk to you about how life can go on after loss if you're ever interested."

I felt my insides bristle. *How lovely that this woman she knows was able to move on and get remarried, but I won't ever get remarried*, I thought. *Peter was the only one for me.* "Thank you for that. If I ever need to talk, I'll let you know. Please tell her I appreciate her offer. Thank you for coming. It means a lot." We said our goodbyes and I watched as she drove away.

Walking back to the house, I suddenly remembered the conversation Peter and I had had the night before he died, the promises I had made to him. I stopped in my tracks. *Oh no. Why did I make promises I knew I couldn't keep?*

◄○►

Monday came like a bucket of cold water thrown in my face. The little bit of closure I felt after the funeral on Saturday had disappeared as quickly as it had appeared. The burial brought its own level of finality that I didn't expect. While I knew it was just his body, the shell of the man he was on earth, the physical act of putting him in the ground was almost unbearable. How had so many women lived through this? I knew I wasn't the first to experience this gut-wrenching process, but the grief seemed to be digging itself deeper and deeper into my soul.

Fern Hill had organized a viewing prior to the burial service, and I desperately needed to get there before that ended. I needed to say one last goodbye before he was gone forever. The kids were arguing and resisting any attempts to get them dressed. They didn't understand what was happening, and didn't want to put on nice clothes *again* and be paraded in front of people *again*. Quite frankly, I didn't blame them one bit, and internally I was on their side. I wanted to shout out, "Let's just put on our sweats, watch movies, and eat junk food all day! Enough with this grief nonsense!" I wanted to ignore reality and stay in the safety of my home.

Instead, we sat down and I explained to them how this service would be different from the one on Saturday. "There won't be as many people—only family and a few friends—and it's in town at the cemetery, not at the church." It was the lamest explanation ever. How does one explain a burial to a five-year-old and a seven-year-old in a way that helps them understand without scaring them? With feet dragging, we once again got dressed, loaded ourselves into my dad's car, and headed out to the cemetery chapel.

Many family members were already there waiting, which was helpful for the kids to see it wasn't just us but not as large a crowd as before. They were comfortable with everyone there and, thankfully, I was too. I pulled several people aside and said, "Please help me for a few minutes. This is very important. I'm going into the viewing, but the kids are not. Please do *not* let them come into the building. I won't allow their last memory of their dad to be of him in a casket. I'll go in alone and when I come out, we'll proceed to his burial." They nodded their confirmation. I turned to see where the kids were and saw them already engaged with family, so quietly slipped through the double doors and into the foyer.

Once in the entryway, I stopped to get my bearings. Everything was quiet and there was a heavy, solemn feeling hanging in the air. The silence allowed me a moment to take a deep breath while I observed the dark furniture and dark-toned carpet. Comfortable chairs with little boxes of tissues next to them and tall green plants filled the space. While it felt solemn, it was also very calming.

Facing the chapel entrance where the double doors were propped open, I could see part of the casket set up for viewing. Patty and Daryl walked out holding each other. I walked toward them, and we embraced. I could feel the weight of their grief as it settled on top of my own, making it almost impossible for my legs to move. They felt cemented in place. Patty and Daryl stepped back and joined the rest of the family outside. We didn't exchange any words. None were adequate for the moment. We felt each other's pain and, through that, a thousand words were silently exchanged.

I took a breath, steadied myself, and walked into the chapel, closing the doors behind me. I needed privacy. I couldn't handle being on display anymore and wanted to be able to speak freely. I stood at the back of the chapel for a few moments as I worked through the memories of attending Peter's thirteen-year-old cousin Jason's service ten years prior. I had stood in the same spot, honoring Jason's memory and kissing his forehead before he was laid to rest, and now, here I was doing the same with my husband. How was this even possible, and how could I move on from this?

I reminded myself this was just his shell as I stood facing the casket, but it didn't help. I slowly approached the front of the chapel, attempting to slow my breath as I saw his body, so still, in the clothes I'd picked out knowing how much he'd hate them. I momentarily regretted that choice, but he looked good in them, so I let the regret fall away with ease. I leaned in so I could speak in a whisper, pretending he was able to hear me. "I remember what I promised, and I'll do everything I can to keep them. I'll do everything in my power to raise our babies well and keep them safe. They'll know how much you love them."

Time stood still as I relayed details from his service to him, when suddenly there came a soft knock at the door. I turned and, through sorrowful swollen eyes, saw the director enter and quietly walk toward me. He apologized for intruding, but needed to let me know it was time to head up the hill for the burial. I nodded and turned to Peter giving my final farewell, with a kiss on the forehead.

As I passed the director on my way out, I grabbed his arm. "Please don't close it until I'm gone." This kind man assured me he wouldn't, and I turned and walked away, leaving my best friend behind.

◄○►

We made our way up the hill to Peter's burial spot. I could see the canopy and chairs set up and Pastor Ness already there waiting. Bless that man for all the funerals and burials he has had to conduct over the years. It can't be easy, and I was thankful for his willingness to be there that day. My dad pulled the car as close as he could and helped the kids and me out. I grabbed their hands, reminding them that we were together, and we walked to the chairs where Pastor Ness motioned for us to sit. As everyone gathered, I kept my eyes on the casket. I couldn't handle making eye contact with anyone. I heard the sniffles from those around me and they echoed off each other like cries in a valley bouncing off the hillsides. I did my best to just maintain my composure. *I'm tired of crying in front of people. I'm deciding right now that after this, I'm done crying in public.*

I'm sure some lovely things were being said, but so many memories were replaying in my mind that I couldn't hear the words being spoken. My mind drifted off to days on the boat working hard but loving life, trips to the river to beat the summer heat, and the snuggles on the sofa that last night with Peter's arms wrapped around the kids before bed. I knew we were close to the end because I heard Pastor reading Psalm 23 and asking everyone to help close with the song I'd chosen. I instantly regretted my choice of "Amazing Grace." *I love this song and now I'll never be able to hear it without being reminded of this moment. Did I just ruin it for my kids too?* I didn't even know how many people were singing because my thoughts drowned out everything around me. In the midst of the singing, I heard again the promise I'd been given just five days before being whispered to my soul: *Don't worry - I have a plan.*

Those words, though few, held such an impact in that very moment. The heaviness of the ceremony that left me feeling lost was changed with that small reminder. I didn't need to know what I was going to do. God told me not to worry because He had a plan, and He always keeps His promises.

The pastor thanked everyone for being there, and I briefly contemplated staying in that spot forever or just climbing on top of the casket as they lowered it into the ground. I felt it was a valid option. Instead, I stood up, took my kids by the hand, and silently walked to the car while others remained behind. I couldn't stay and watch.

Don't worry - I have a plan. I had a new confidence in those simple words spoken to me. My focus was on my kids, our future, and finding a way to keep my promises to Peter.

CHAPTER 14

I'm Grieving as Fast as I Can

The week following the funeral was exceptionally difficult. I was reminded daily that he was no longer with us. His truck would never roll up the driveway. His humor would never lighten the mood in our home and neither would his laughter. I'd never hear him tell me how much he loved me or how beautiful I was—as he'd done every day we were together. As I moved about my days, I realized that while I was stuck in this feeling of shock and horror, everybody else had gone back to living their lives as they had before.

Friends and family returned to their homes, their responsibilities, and their normal lives. Yet I was still here counting every minute I was having to live without him. *How can people just go back to living like nothing happened? Don't they realize my world is still shattered?* Of course, they did, but I couldn't see that because of where my heart was. I wanted everyone to stop and stay frozen in time. *Why can't we just stop time until I can find my footing? What if I never find my footing?*

So many beautiful souls who sensed our needs showed up. I realize now that many people needed to help not just because it was the right thing to do, but because it helped them work through their own grief. We're created for community, designed to help each other and this is never more evident than in times of tragedy. The connection they felt to

Peter and me and the kids was deep. They were hurt by his passing, and by helping us they were also helping themselves. Providing for a specific need in our life brought them a sense of purpose and helped to heal their broken hearts.

The phone rang one afternoon as I sat at my dining room table writing thank-you notes to all the people who'd sent food, gifts, flowers, or just heartfelt notes to the kids and me, and my mom ran to answer it. She came around the corner saying, "Jodee is on the phone. She's in town and wants to know what you need. She'll pick it up and bring it by."

"I don't need anything. Tell her thank you, but I don't need anything right now." My mom walked away, then came back. "She says she needs to get something for you. What do you need?" I felt slightly annoyed because I didn't need anything, but as I paused trying to think of an excuse, the look on Mom's face said, *Be kind and think of something quickly.*

"How about some laundry soap? She can bring me some laundry soap," I said dismissively.

Mom came back into the room satisfied with the exchange and said Jodee would be dropping it off in a bit. At least I had some time to check my attitude before my expected company arrived. It was clear that being able to provide something for me brought a bit of joy to Jodee. She was grieving as well, and I believe knowing she could provide some small support helped her with her feeling of loss.

I gained an understanding from that exchange that while I felt, and still feel, my pain on a much deeper level, I wasn't alone. Did that bring comfort? Not in an "I'm glad others are hurting too" way, but in the sense that my grief wasn't a solitary experience. There might not have been other widows or widowers reaching out to me, but there were others hurting and sharing in my pain, and there was comfort in that knowledge. I remembered hearing somewhere that not accepting help or a gift from someone was stealing a blessing from them. My independent nature had to be put aside to allow others not only to bless me with their help but hopefully to be blessed themselves.

Don't Worry—I Have a Plan.

God sent the best people at the right times to be a part of my healing process. Some had simple words of encouragement on days when I felt I couldn't continue. Others were there to talk about anything other than the tragedy I'd just endured, which was exactly what I needed. I didn't want to spend every day talking about my feelings, because there were so many days that I just felt terrible. Who wants to talk about feeling terrible every day? Give me something "normal" to talk about. Anything. Let's talk about baseball schedules, birthday parties, and end-of-school-year craziness.

Many times, at the grocery store or bank I'd see someone spot me and instantly it was a tilt of the head, furrowed brows, droopy eyes, and a frown instead of a smile. I could hear the words before they were spoken: *How are you doing?* With each word drawn out and dripping with sympathy. Sometimes there was a *dear* or *you poor thing* added at the end, but always the head tilt and the dreaded question.

I hated how I wanted to respond when this happened. I hated that my first thought was to turn and run the other way or scream, "I'm falling apart! How do you think I'm doing?!" These were kind people who genuinely wanted to show they cared, and I just wanted to avoid them. I imagine if they didn't show they cared, I'd have been offended and wondered what was wrong with them. My emotions were unstable and unpredictable at best.

When greeted with the tilted head, I'd politely respond with, "I'm okay. Thank you for asking." There were a couple of times when I was too tired to control myself and my snarky, overly cheerful voice took over. I'd say something like, "I'm great! How are you?" Or "You know, things are going so well. How's life treating you?" I know it wasn't kind, but after a while it got more difficult to pretend and, honestly, someone who's recently experienced a tragic loss isn't doing well—so please stop asking how we're doing and skip to the next topic.

Ask questions that aren't related to feelings. Ask about the last T-ball or baseball game or any athletic event. Ask if there are any travel plans or if there's a new hobby. Ask about the latest movie or the last fun book we've read. Invite us for dinner or coffee or to go for a walk. Sometimes, what we need is to be asked anything that feels normal and not related to sadness and grief. Or just share something that's happening in your life and then allow space for us to share in return.

I remember a significant moment in the days following Peter's death when I wasn't asked how I was. I wasn't given a head tilt or an apologetic look. I was offered raw, honest comfort by a friend who didn't apologize but shared her heart. I was at home trying to focus on completing at least one task when there was a knock at my door. It was my dear friend Jennifer. She stood there with tears in her eyes as she thrust a silver fabric book bag toward me. "I didn't know what to do. I went to the bookstore but didn't know which book to get, so I got them all." This incredible woman drove over an hour to the bookstore to buy books on losing a loved one and surviving loss as well as books and workbooks for kids who've lost a parent. I had no words to express the immense amount of appreciation for her. I just took the bag and hugged her as the tears began to spill over.

Those books sat in that silver bag on the floor next to the sofa for a couple of months and stared at me every time I walked by. I was torn—I wanted to read them but wasn't ready to deal with my emotions. A huge part of me just wanted to crawl into bed and never breathe again, but it was impossible to ignore that shiny bag as it sat almost mocking me: *You can continue to try and do this on your own, or you can pick up one of these books and gain some tools that may help you.* One night after the kids had gone to bed, I begrudgingly grabbed the bag and sat on the sofa.

I thumbed through every book and, in the end, one caught my attention: *I'm Grieving as Fast as I Can: How Young Widows and Widowers Can Cope and Heal* by Linda Feinberg. I liked the title because it called out young widows, and the "as fast as I can" part gave me a feeling of control over my process. At first, I just skimmed the book. I mocked and criticized the stories, thinking of them as victims and not respecting what they'd experienced because they were "getting over it," which was crazy because their stories were exactly what I was going through—I just couldn't admit it. I wasn't able to process in that moment that "as fast as I can" didn't mean "quickly."

Don't Worry—I Have a Plan.

Months later when I was able to sit and thoroughly read the book, the message became clear. Grieving as fast as I could wasn't about getting over the grief or working through the emotions quickly so I could move on. It was about acknowledging what I'd experienced and moving through the emotions at my own pace. *I'm grieving as fast as I can. This is my grief and I get to do it at my pace.*

This book gave me permission to stop listening to all the advice from those around me and just do the grief thing the way I needed to. I didn't need anyone else's permission to do what I knew I needed for me and my kids and to do it in our timing. Grieving could be between me and God and nobody else. This was incredible! I felt immense freedom and relief.

This was a pivotal point in my healing, and I felt I was able to start moving forward with the promises I'd made to Peter. I could be keeping my promises and still be grieving. I didn't have to "get over him" or be done grieving to be able to move on. If I waited until I got over him or completed my grieving process, I'd never do anything again for the rest of my life. That book gave me permission to continue processing my grief while simultaneously taking steps forward to a new normal. What an incredible gift!

I knew it wouldn't be easy, but I started to understand that the promises I'd made to Peter weren't a negative after all but a gift. I was given the gift of knowing exactly what Peter wanted me to do: he wanted me to live my life to the fullest, and he wanted his kids to be happy and taken care of. This doesn't mean I didn't struggle with making many decisions, but the three most important ones were made for me.

I needed to take steps to keep moving forward so I wouldn't get stuck. I needed to figure out what steps I could take first. What would be attainable when everything felt so monumental?

While watching one of the kids' soccer practices, my friend Jodee quietly asked, "Are you still sleeping on the sofa?" I confirmed I was. "Stephanie, it's been five months—you can't sleep on the sofa forever." Sleeping in my bed sounded horrendous. I couldn't bear the thought of sleeping in it without Peter. It was our bed and it felt cold and lonely without him. I told her I didn't think I could do it. She showed great kindness in the way she offered suggestions. "Why don't you try rearranging the furniture and buying all new bedding. Pillows, sheets, comforter—all of it. Make it all new." She offered to come over to help, but in those moments, it became clear this first step needed to be mine to accomplish. I told her I'd figure it out, and she again strongly encouraged me to follow through.

It took me a week but, with all new bedding in hand, I rearranged the furniture so the room took on a different look, and started to sleep in the bed again. Well . . . not immediately, but eventually I made it through a whole night, and that one accomplishment felt like I'd crossed a huge hurdle. It gave me the strength to move on to the next task.

CHAPTER 15

Promise #1

"I want you to move if you can. I don't want the kids growing up here without me. I love our home and I love our friends, but I won't be here."

My first promise to Peter was a difficult one to keep because Westport was and always would be my home. That community, which while still in high school I was desperate to leave, was now the only place I wanted to be. It was our home, our comfort zone. Leaving would be agonizing, but I'd made a promise. Peter didn't want his kids to be raised in his hometown without him.

After some of the dust had settled, Peter's parents came by and presented me with a plan they'd discussed and were going to start implementing. They'd purchased a piece of property and were in the process of building a house on it for themselves. "There's enough room for us to add a small house for you and the kids. We're ready to go to the county right away to get the permitting process started." They felt it would be best to have us close so they could help with the kids, and then I wouldn't have to maintain an old house on my own. I was taken aback by this unexpected presentation and the generous gift they wanted to give. "Think on it and we can discuss plans in the next day or so."

I went to bed that night contemplating this proposition. What an incredible gift they were offering me. I could see all the benefits it would provide. I wouldn't be alone, and I'd have constant help with the kids.

I wouldn't be in a house that needed repairs I wasn't physically able to manage myself. The list went on. However, something was preventing me from jumping at the opportunity, and I needed time to pray and process why I was hesitating.

When I talked with Patty and Daryl about my decision, I chose my words very carefully. Saying the wrong thing could create unnecessary and unwanted barriers in our relationship. "I'm overwhelmed by your extremely generous offer," I said. "It's so enticing, and I can see all the ways it would benefit me and the kids, but I need to decline." I knew where their hearts were coming from, but needed to create my own home with the kids. They insisted it would be my home and I'd have my own space, but I knew that, in time, boundary lines would blur. I needed to keep family close, but not so close that the kids would be confused as to who the parent was. "I'm going to stay in my house, and we'll be okay. The kids and I are now the family and I believe this is the path we need to take."

I could tell they were surprised, disappointed, and a little offended by what I was saying because what they offered was a huge gift and one not too many widows would be given, but they graciously accepted my answer and never mentioned it again. I was grateful they didn't continue to bring it up, because I know I'd have caved in and gone along with their plan to make them happy—and doing so would have required me to break my promise to Peter. This is how I know in the depths of my soul that God was giving me the strength to stand on my own. I never would have been able to do it by myself.

I felt I could put this one promise off for a while. Peter didn't give timelines when I made the promises, so I felt I had the freedom to choose the timing. However, the feeling of having unfinished business kept gnawing at me, so I started my search for where we could move. I perused houses within a ninety-mile radius. I thought if I could be out of town but still close enough to make it a day trip for visits, that would be a good distance. I searched and visited several places for months and eventually found a cute little house in a good area that was about an hour's drive away.

Don't Worry—I Have a Plan.

I started to get excited at the thought of a fresh start in a place where I wouldn't be haunted by memories. I had two living replicas of Peter with me every day named Perry and Sarah, which was such a gift and they kept me alive, but needed to let some of the other visual reminders go. At least for a time. I knew that sitting in a Peter shrine day after day wasn't going to be a healthy healing environment.

The cute little house with yellow paint had a small backyard, was perfectly situated in a quaint neighborhood, and was right in my price range. It was in the country a bit, but not so far that I couldn't take advantage of the amenities we'd find helpful nearby. *Good schools, good neighborhood, great price. Let's take a look!*

Isn't it interesting how you can be making strides toward a goal, feeling you're making all the right decisions and then suddenly God comes in and nudges with a smile saying, "That's a nice plan, but I have a different plan and was thinking we'd move in this direction instead."

What?! Are you kidding me?

Before I was able to look at this cute little house God redirected me. In His gentle manner, He started directing me along a path that would allow me to keep two promises with one decision.

God carried me through every step of this journey. When I doubted myself, He whispered the reminder that He had a plan. When I felt overwhelmed, He sent peace. When I had a need, He sent someone to fulfill it. When I felt alone, He held me.

I confided in a friend how alone I felt and how I just longed to be held by loving, comforting arms. A lot of people were hugging me, but it wasn't the same. Her response? "Pray about it. Ask for it and believe it will be given." I did just that. Every day. Then one day I woke up realizing I'd dreamed all night that I was resting in the most loving arms. I woke up feeling so comforted, and the feeling of loneliness I'd felt the day before was gone. Ask and believe it will be given.

CHAPTER 16

———

The LULAS

A few days after Peter's burial, I received a call from my general manager, George, asking if we could meet for lunch and talk about the
timeframe for me to return to work. We set a date, and I started to worry
about the expectations of the company. I had a lot of respect for George
and wanted to return to work to fulfill my duties, but knew I wasn't in a
mental or emotional place to do so.

I allowed my anxiety to take over before George and I even met. I
convinced myself they were either going to make me return to work right
away or were going to let me go. I couldn't not work, but didn't know
how I could possibly be a productive member of the team at that point.
I didn't even know how I was going to work the same job with the same
demand and be able to take care of the kids. I was a single mom now and
needed to put the kids first, which would mean no more working overtime or even weekends whenever possible.

Was I going to need to find a new job? How could I communicate my
needs without sounding selfish or too needy? *It will be okay. Everything
will be fine*, I told myself as I set out for my lunch meeting.

When I arrived at the restaurant, George was already there and had
respectfully chosen a table in the back corner, away from prying eyes. I
was able to sit facing away from anyone in the restaurant and was thankful for that. I sat across from George, wringing my hands beneath the
table, searching his face for a sign of what might be coming my way. We

exchanged some small talk, ordered some food, and then he looked at me and said, "We've been discussing the best way to help you transition back to work." I could feel my heart rate increasing. I held my breath. *Please, God, help me stay strong.*

George folded his hands on the table and looked at me seriously. "You mean a lot to the company, and we care about you and your kids, and want to make sure you're being taken care of."

I felt my emotions threatening to breach the barricade I'd built and spill over my eyes and down my cheeks.

"Stephanie, what do you need? What do you want to come back to? We realize this is a tremendous life change for you and we want to be supportive of you and the kids. So, you name it. What do you need?"

Relief and utter astonishment.

Oh, I wasn't expecting this. I don't know how long the silence was, but it must have been longer than I thought because George encouraged me to take my time and let him know later if I needed to.

I took a deep breath, said a silent prayer, and told him I knew what I needed. "I can't return to the same job. I need to be present as a mom for my kids. This is more than becoming a single mom and trying to balance a schedule. This is about making sure I'm present for them while we work through our loss."

Then I waited, expecting, "Well, we don't know if we can do that," which would have been acceptable. Instead, I got, "Okay, we can do that. You let us know when you're ready to come back, and we'll have something for you."

What did he just say? I was stunned. I couldn't believe the gift I'd just been handed. How did I get so blessed to work for a company that cared this much for their employees? They were willing to give me the gift of time to figure out what my life was now. Not only the gift of time but the gift of a change of position to make myself available to my children. I needed to do my best to get back to work as soon as possible. I didn't want to take advantage of their generosity: I needed to make sure I was getting things in order so I could return. I didn't know what they had in store for me, but if it meant I could be available for my kids, I'd do it.

If they wanted me to clean rooms or pick up trash, I was their gal. I was so incredibly relieved by their generosity that I wasn't going to be picky.

I took a month to handle all the paperwork that had become a full-time job itself; and, when I felt the affairs were in order, decided I needed to go back to work. I didn't want to take any more time, and being sad didn't feel like an adequate reason to not go back. One of my coworkers called and I told her I'd be back at the office the next day. Getting back into a routine with the kids might be a challenge, but we'd make it work. We had to. I felt like there was no other choice.

I was able to successfully get myself up, get the kids ready, and drop them off at school before heading to the office. But once the kids were out of the car I could feel my mask slipping. I'd become very good at keeping my immensely deep grief hidden from the kids so I could focus on taking care of them, but once they were out of sight, I could feel the emotions creeping up toward my eyes. I was nervous to face people and try to keep my mask in place all day. *I can do this*, I kept repeating to myself, and prayed all the way from the school to the office.

I pulled into the parking lot and put the car in park. I sat there for a moment and gave myself one more pep talk. *It's been enough time. I'm fine. Things are fine and I'm ready to go back to work.* I took a deep breath and slowly peeled my fingers away from the steering wheel, turned the car off, and removed the keys from the ignition. I grabbed my purse and got out of the car. When I turned around, my coworker was standing there waiting for me. She'd seen me arrive and had come out of the office to greet me. As my eyes met hers, I felt the mask I'd just worked so hard to keep in place melt and slide away. I shook my head and whispered, "I can't do this. I'm not ready." Then the tears took control.

She hugged me and cried with me while I fell apart in the middle of the parking lot. She was so compassionate. "It's okay. You don't have to do this right now." She told me to go home and try again another day. Everyone was so supportive and wanted me to do what I needed to take care of myself and the kids. I felt guilty for not being able to manage myself yet grateful for these incredibly generous people I was working for.

When I was able to stop crying, I poured myself back into my car, put the keys back into the ignition, and started the car again. Gripping the steering wheel, with my shoulders slumped and my head bowed, I prayed, "God, help me be able to live without this heaviness of grief." I couldn't go to work, but I didn't want to go home and be alone. I also couldn't bring myself to drive to the cemetery and sit until it was time to pick the kids up from school. Driving to the cemetery had become a part of my daily routine. I'd get to the entrance and turn on my fight song, "Praise You in This Storm," by Casting Crowns, and would sing as much as I could as I climbed the hill to Peter's resting place. Then I'd sit or sometimes lie next to him until it was time to pick up the kids or run errands.

I knew I needed to break myself from that routine, but if I couldn't stay at work, what would I do instead?

I continued praying, asking God to show me what to do, and remembered the coffee cup planter with flowers and the open invitation from Andrea and Malynnda: "We meet for coffee every morning. Join us when you're ready."

"Thank you, God." I decided to be brave and test out these old friends to see if they meant it when they said I could join them. I dialed Malynnda's number and, when she answered, told her I couldn't go to work and asked if the invitation for coffee was still open. She answered with a quick "Yep. We're here so come on over." I had no idea what I was hoping for and no expectations of what I might find, but knew it was where I was supposed to be. I never could have dreamed of the lifelong blessing that would come from that open invitation.

When I walked in, I saw Andrea sitting on a barstool at the kitchen counter with coffee in hand and her Bible open on the counter. Malynnda was standing on the opposite side of the counter. "Come on in," she said. "Coffee cups are in this cupboard, and cream and sugar are over here. You can help yourself or I can do it for you. Your choice." I grabbed a cream-colored mug with a forest scene that included a large whitetail deer on it, poured some coffee, and added enough cream and sugar that the coffee flavor didn't have a fighting chance of making it to my tastebuds. In that moment, I silently congratulated myself for being able to make a decision, as small as it was.

I don't know what they'd been discussing, and don't remember if I even joined in the conversation. I'm sure I brought the temperature of the room down as I sat with my sad self just feeling thankful to be in their company. They were respectful and just let me be. No questions and no expectations as they continued their morning routine.

I joined them daily for coffee and found their company slowly replenishing my parched soul. Some days we'd get our friend Tina on speakerphone (these were the days before FaceTime) to visit with us. These ladies slowly filled my well with the love they poured over me and my kids.

As the days wore on, we shared more than coffee. We shared our souls, realizing each of us brought something different to the friendship. We each had a gift the others didn't have, and began to realize how nicely we fitted together—like each of us was a piece of one larger puzzle.

Andrea, the no-nonsense friend, asked the hard questions and gave the tough love responses when we needed them. Tina, the planner, was able to get us all together for BBQs and holiday gatherings. When she planned something, we showed up. We knew if we didn't, she'd come find us and we'd get an earful. Malynnda, the encourager and easiest to tease shared her love and compassion through thoughtful words and tears of empathy. I didn't quite know what role I played in the group, but was thankful they were willing to keep me, because I needed them.

We found that having our families together, while difficult to schedule, was an effortless task once all were in proximity. Our kids miraculously got on well and we were able to flow through events with one of us seamlessly picking up where another left off. There was never a lack of conversation, and the laughter we shared made our bellies ache and was medicine to my soul.

It was with their encouragement that I was able to return to work and ease back into a manageable routine. My employer was patient, allowing me to sit at the reception desk and answer phones until I felt I was ready to take on more. While answering phones was something I could do in my sleep, I found the work to be taxing when I first returned. It didn't take long, though, before I felt I was able to accept more responsibility.

Eventually, they moved me into a human resources position, which felt like a great fit, and I was grateful.

Returning to work meant I was no longer able to attend morning coffee, and my friends and I were all on very different work schedules, so finding time to be together was a challenge. I was disappointed the days the others were all together but I was at work. I wanted to be present and a part of whatever they were doing. One day when they'd all taken a drive to Olympia for lunch, I did my best to be a part of it by participating in a group text. They kept me apprised of their whereabouts and what entertaining events were taking place so I could feel like I was with them. When my lunchtime ended and I was returning to work, I signed off with "LULAS" (Love U Like A Sister).

I found out later that this had caused much confusion with one of them, who kept reading it over and over but couldn't figure out what I meant by "LULAS." This resulted in the other two falling into hysterics every time she read it out loud. They understood, but she kept struggling to understand. After they recounted this story to me, I decided it was a done deal. We'd officially be The LULAS.

The LULAS gained another member through the years. Mandy, the helper, completes a missing piece of the puzzle with her enormous, caring heart. Her ability to see a need and fill it or give directions on how it needs to be filled is a gift to all of us. We're stronger and better because of each other. Some people think our friendship just happened, but we know it didn't. We'd known each other for most of our lives, but our individual friendships looked different than when we all came together. We know we have something special in each other, and work hard to preserve what we have. We practice unconditional love. We accept each other for who we are with no intention of trying to change each other or shape someone into what we want them to be. We value what the others bring to the relationship, knowing we each need that gift of wisdom, wit, compassion, and love.

We're each other's biggest cheerleaders when we need encouragement and softest landings when times are tough. We drop what we're doing when one of us is in need. When Tina's dad passed away, the three of us who were in town grabbed groceries and went to her house. We restocked her fridge, did the laundry, put fresh linens on the beds, scrubbed the bathrooms and floors, and organized the silverware drawer. When Andrea's husband was in the hospital, we did the same: scrubbed toilets, washed linens, cleaned dishes, and mopped floors. I don't share this to be boastful, although it would be easy for me to boast about my friends. I share this because this is what it means to have a sisterhood—a community of friends. We work for this friendship and this friendship works for us.

In a time when I needed compassion, patience, and grace, they gave it to me, but when I started to veer into self-pity, they gave me a good dose of "Get up. Remember who you are and who you belong to and stop the wallowing." They kept me going and rallied around me when I needed it most.

I was the tree that was standing alone, and they were the forest that grew up around me and protected me from the storm.

CHAPTER 17

Woman! Make Me a Sandwich!

In the months following Peter's death, people would say to my son Perry, "You're the man of the house now." That statement triggered instant, blood-boiling rage in me every time I heard it. I'd try to gently correct the bearer of the inappropriate message. "He isn't the man of the house. He's seven years old and has many years of being a child before he's the man of any house, let alone this one." (Oh, the irony you'll find in this statement later.) The look I'd get from some people told me they didn't agree. A few apologized, but the apology was too late because the words were already spoken and couldn't be unheard by my son, who started to believe he was indeed the "man of the house."

In early fall when there was a crispness to the air, the kids were outside playing and I was adding wood to the woodstove to take the chill out of the house. Perry came inside and stood nearby watching me. Suddenly, with an arrogant tone he said, "Woman, make me a sandwich." A deafening silence fell across the room.

Peter would tease me by saying that occasionally. He never called me "woman" in any way other than jest. Whenever he said, "Woman, make me a sandwich," he always did it with a smirk on his face and a twinkle in his eye. He knew it would trigger some light banter between us and we'd laugh, but our son had no idea of the intent with which his dad had said it. He felt he was the man of the house now; therefore, he should call me "woman." Oh dear.

I turned and looked at him. "I'm sorry, what did you just call me?"

My seven-year-old boy's eyes got large as he realized he'd made a mistake. I could see him trying to figure out how to back out of this hole he'd so quickly dug. He whispered, "I heard Dad say that to you before . . ."

My heart was hurting at the mention of his dad, yet I was still fuming over what he'd said to me. I was more upset with the people who'd convinced him he needed to step into this role that wasn't appropriate for him, but needed to address the confused child in front of me.

I squatted down so I could be at eye level with him and tried to speak calmly. "Well, Dad never said it the way you just did, and he was always teasing. You'll not call me that again. I know people have told you you're now the man of the house, but you're still a kid, and you'll remain a kid until you officially become an adult, in age, later. I'm officially relieving you of your duties as man of the house. There's only one adult under this roof and that's me, your mother, and you'll treat me with respect. Do you understand me?"

I received a very slow, silent head nod in response and sent him outside to play as kids are supposed to do. The tears flowed as I made him a sandwich and contemplated how I was ever going to do this on my own.

My patience and will were running out quickly. I needed help.

◄o►

Before I embarked on the extremely scary process of fulfilling my promises, I made the decision that the kids and I would start counseling. I knew they were experiencing emotions they weren't sharing with me. Perry had taken on the natural role of protector, and Sarah didn't know how to express her feelings in any way other than anger. I was dealing with my own emotions and knew I didn't have the capacity to work through my grief as well as help the kids work through theirs. I'd tried to use the books my friend had given us, but wasn't strong enough to help the kids to do the exercises. So, off to counseling we went.

Don't Worry—I Have a Plan.

I had a list of counselors in our area and started working down the list making phone calls and inquiring about appointments. I didn't know how the kids would respond, so sat them down and explained what a counselor was and what their role would be in helping us. "They aren't going to tell us we're crazy or that something is wrong with us, and they aren't going to push us to do things we aren't ready to do. They're just going to help us work through how we feel about losing your dad and find ways to help us feel better." I didn't even know if what I was telling them was accurate, but it sounded good in my head. So, I went with it.

It took a little while for us to find the right counselor. I felt it was important that we all agreed on who we'd see because we needed to do this together. We all needed individual care, but also needed to work together as a family. We'd visit one counselor and I'd like them but one of the kids wouldn't feel comfortable, or one of the kids would like them but I wasn't comfortable.

After a few unsuccessful appointments, I shared with my friend Tina how taxing the process was and that I wasn't sure we'd find one we all liked or felt comfortable with. "I just heard of someone nearby who recently opened her own practice. She's more mature, in that she has adult age children, and I've heard she's kind and welcoming."

"Send me her information. We'll give her a try."

I picked the kids up early from school one day and drove forty-five minutes to the small, unassuming office of this new counselor. We walked in and were welcomed by soft lights and comfortable seating that felt more like a living room than an office space. So far, I liked the setup, and the kids didn't seem apprehensive.

As we were taking in the scene, the counselor walked out of her office and greeted us. She was lovely, with shoulder-length brown hair, a crisp white blouse, and a kind smile that spread from the corners of her mouth up to her eyes. I instantly felt at ease. After she introduced herself to all of us, the kids looked at me and I knew we'd found the right one. I could feel the tension fall off my shoulders and was thankful to be there.

We had weekly appointments for a while, then tapered to every other week. The counselor would meet with the kids separately, then give them a project to work on either individually or together. She had a room for kids set up with all sorts of games, toys, and therapy-related tools adjacent to her regular counseling office. After she gave the kids their assignment, she'd meet with me in a space that was private yet still within sight of where the kids were. It was nice that we could meet and work while the kids were close but not close enough to hear our conversations.

I'm thankful for the time we spent with the counselor. Not just because we needed to work through the big emotions we were feeling, but also because it provided, through time, the validation we needed that we were healing and moving in the right direction. At one point I shared a struggle I was having and my thoughts on how to handle it and the counselor responded, "Well, it appears you're doing well with making decisions." It was the affirmation I needed. Perry and Sarah seemed more open to talk to me about how they were feeling instead of tiptoeing around my emotions. Sarah especially started using words to help me understand how she was feeling instead of bursting into fits of angry screaming. Her periods of happiness seemed to last longer and this brought more peace to my heart.

I appreciated that our counselor would talk to the kids and ask them what they were okay with her sharing with me. I knew there would be things they'd try to protect me from, but also things they might be scared to tell me because they didn't know how I'd react, and that was okay. I didn't need to know everything they were thinking and feeling—I just needed to know they were talking to someone who could help. Even if that person wasn't me.

As we continued with counseling, I could see and feel how each of us was benefiting individually and together as a family. I was starting to believe we really would be okay. I was gaining confidence that we could do this new way of life without Peter, and we could do it well. It felt like a small drop of salve had been placed on my raw, damaged heart.

CHAPTER 18

Single Parenting

It took me a little over a month to be able to return to work. I wasn't ready to return but didn't want to take advantage of the generosity given by my employer. I was thankful that our customers were so kind to me. I knew I looked like a shell of who I was before, but they didn't comment on how I looked. They just offered condolences and support, which was more than I could have asked for.

We'd done our best to get back in the groove of school and life, but it wasn't easy. I wasn't what I'd consider the best mom through this process. Always putting the kids first with my decisions, taking them to counseling, and protecting them from events and information I thought might hurt them makes me sound like I had it all together, but I didn't. I was a hot mess before it was considered a cute cliché to be one. I did my best, but my best certainly wasn't good enough. I knew it and the kids knew it. I just didn't know how to change it.

I felt like a rope that was frayed up to the very last inch as I tried to manage the house, work, kids, and school. I'd seamlessly and unconsciously transitioned from a deeply grieving, hugging, and loving mom to a yelling and screaming mom who couldn't control her emotions—especially when the kids weren't doing what I asked them to do. Or when they were fighting with each other. Or pretty much when I was awake and breathing. I was so worn out emotionally that I lost all ability to respond to their behavior in an appropriate manner. So, I yelled. I hated myself and felt deep guilt every time I yelled, but couldn't seem to find a way to stop or change how I was responding either.

While counseling was helping me with my grief, we hadn't had a chance to get to the parenting tools I needed. One day I was approached by Mrs. Sperline, an elementary school teacher and family friend. "Stephanie," she said with her quiet, warmhearted voice. "I've heard Perry make some comments about how his mom yells a lot lately."

The guilt rushed over me like scorching water.

"I thought that with everything you've been through, you might be interested in this class we're offering. It's Parenting with Love and Logic, and provides some great tools to help take back control without having to raise your voice. We've taken the class as teachers, but now a few of us are taking it as parents. Do you want to think about it and let me know? Childcare is provided and we'd love to have you join us."

My first internal reaction was, *Oh, so you think I'm a terrible parent?*

My second, *Oh my gosh, my kids are telling everyone I'm a horrible parent.*

And then, *I'm desperate for help and I'll do anything to not damage my kids anymore and get some emotional relief for myself. Please, please, please help me!*

I looked at this lovely, deeply kind woman and after contemplating all the ways I could respond, said, "Thank you. If you give me the information, I'll think about it." I was desperate but didn't want to come across as desperate. My pride needed to be preserved.

I took the information home and read more about the class. I had a lot of respect for Mrs. Sperline and for the other teacher facilitating the class. As I read more about the tools I'd gain by attending, I decided it was my best chance to become a better mom for my kids. What I was doing wasn't working for any of us. I needed to try something different, and this class might be exactly what I needed.

The class was a godsend and I'm thankful I decided to attend. It was a welcoming environment with other parents and teachers who were aiming for the same goal: to be better for our kids. The tools I gained—such as using experiences as opportunities for learning and offering appropriate choices for each situation—helped me parent Sarah and Perry in a way that was tailored to their personalities and learning styles, and it took the responsibility of consequences for choices made off me and put it back on them.

The first night of class I went home and started implementing some of the tools I'd learned. I was surprised at how quickly it worked. I didn't yell during bedtime. I gave choices that were fair to me and appropriate for the kids. Instead of fighting about each step of the bedtime routine, I offered options, giving them a feeling of control—and it worked! The options were simple, such as, "What do you want to do first? Put on your pajamas or brush your teeth?" I was so relieved that, after the kids went to bed, I sat on the sofa and relished the victory over bedtime battles. I finally had the tools I needed to be a better mom.

We still battled, but in time I gained enough tools and confidence that I was able to address each situation with a new perspective and feeling of calm. I now felt I had better control over my emotions, which made a huge difference to the overall outcome.

The tools and feeling of calm were evident when Sarah got herself out of her car seat while we were driving along the highway. I pulled over, asked her to get back into her seat, but she refused. We sat on the side of the highway for thirty minutes with me increasing the volume of my music to drown out her yelling while I waited for her to get back into her car seat because I refused to physically force her. I waited through the outburst and won without raising my voice, *and* she never escaped her car seat again.

I think the hardest part of this experience was setting aside my pride and admitting I was struggling with parenting on my own and needed some help. Attending the class with people I knew was challenging, but I decided if they were there then they were trying to be better parents as well, and what a great thing to be a part of. I'm forever grateful for Mrs. Sperline and her willingness to see I was struggling, to reach out to me in love and kindness—not in judgment—and to offer help.

As I've reflected on this part of my journey over the years, I've often questioned why it was so difficult for me to make the transition to single parenting. I'd been an on-again, off-again single parent being married to a commercial fisherman, so why was it so difficult? Was it the grief the kids and I were experiencing? Most definitely, but there was more to it. When Peter was alive, even when he was away for work, there was always the promise he'd be coming home. Help would be on the way and relief would be in sight. But he wasn't returning from this absence, and the heaviness of that reality made every situation feel more daunting. I needed the help, and God sent that help through a beautiful soul not being afraid to see my struggle and offer a lifeline. I'm grateful I took it.

If you're struggling with becoming a single parent, you don't need to do this on your own. Find some good support in your area whether through family, friends, neighbors, a local church, or a community group. Find a parenting class or just other people willing to stand by your side and help you. Find *people*. Don't try to do this on your own if you don't have to. All children deserve to have a multitude of people speaking life and love over them. Set aside your pride and let others help you. Even if it's the neighbor for two hours after school on Tuesdays. Ask and allow others to help. Spending time with your children may be the biggest blessing of others' lives as well.

◄◦►

Parenting wasn't the only area I found I was struggling with since Peter's passing. While I was the main manager of our finances when he was alive, I didn't do it alone, and our future felt secure because we were together. Now I felt unsure of how to move forward, planning for my future alone. This was a total shift in mindset, and I needed to find help with this as well.

There are times in our lives when we're allowed to reflect and see how certain events that seemed so insignificant at the time played a much larger role than we could have imagined. In 2005, the year before Peter's death, a friend had invited me to listen to Jim Boora, a financial advisor, talk to a group of women about investing. I had no idea then the significance of the timing of that event.

The presentation sounded like a bore, and I wondered if this guy was needing to fill some sort of presentation quota like they do in multilevel marketing operations. I was busy with work, managing business for the boat, and raising two young kids. I also didn't want to go and sit with a bunch of women I felt socially insignificant around and listen about how I should invest money I didn't have. The ladies were lovely, but I saw my social status as well beneath theirs because I didn't have the house, cars, or clothes they had. I shamed myself for thinking this and ended up making the time to attend. I was doing it for a friend I adored, and she had great respect for Jim. She wanted to make sure his time wasn't wasted with just one or two people in attendance. So, truthfully, I went so there wouldn't be an empty chair in the room.

Who knew that sitting in a small meeting room listening to his presentation would become so important to me later. I listened intently to Jim explain the stock market and the benefits of investing, but his presentation wasn't just about investing in general. He talked about the importance of investing in ourselves and how women specifically don't tend to feel they're important enough to do this for themselves. So true! Considering my marriage to a commercial fisherman carried a significant risk of becoming a widow, I was genuinely interested in investing in myself and my future. I needed to take this seriously and do something to make sure I was in control, because there was a chance I'd need to depend solely on myself.

Unfortunately, I make procrastinating look like child's play. I didn't make an appointment to get my investments started. That is, until I was left sitting with a small life insurance check in my hand. While it was just a piece of paper, it felt like I was holding a thousand-pound brick. The question I'd been asking so much lately came to mind. *What am I supposed to do?*

It occurred to me in that moment that I had to invest in myself. Now was my time to take control and make sure my future was secure. But how? If I'd not gone to that meeting and met Jim Boora, the financial advisor from across the bay, I'd not have known what to do. I was smart enough to know I needed help—I just didn't know exactly how to get that help. I remembered listening to the incredibly kind financial advisor portraying such confidence and instilling an honest belief that each of us in that room was worth his time and worthy of investing in ourselves. I knew with 100-percent certainty that he was the one to help me plan my future.

I felt small as I walked into his office, knowing I was clueless about what I needed. I just knew I needed help. His office felt huge, and his dark cherry desk seemed as large a surface as the building itself. He gave me a warm welcome and invited me to sit in the chair across the giant desk from him. I held in my hand the folder, with different articles of investment literature, he'd given each of us during his presentation and gently set it on his desk. I didn't even know why I'd brought it. It just felt like I should have something larger than a #10 envelope in my hand when meeting with him.

He reintroduced himself to me and I obliged him with the courteous small talk that was still so painful for me to manage. When he asked how he could help me, I said, "I'm here because I was impressed with your presentation at the Tokeland Hotel months ago. I appreciated your earnestness regarding women investing in themselves. I lost my husband on April 19 and need some help." *Lost my husband. What does that even mean? He isn't lost. He's dead. Why do we use this phrase, and why can't I say it without feeling like I'm going to be sick? I need to strike this from my repertoire.*

He folded his hands on his desk and leaned forward: "I'm so sorry for your loss, Stephanie. This can't be easy for you and I'm so glad you came in today. How can I help?"

With my hands sweating and shaking, I pulled the check from my handbag. My mouth went dry, and I could feel the fear and grief rising in my throat and across my cheeks in red flames as I silently begged the tears to cooperate today. *Please just give me one day to be able to articulate my needs without your watery presence!* They didn't cooperate. They couldn't have cared less about me and my need for decorum. I barely spoke the words as I gently slid the check across the desk to Jim. "I have this, and I need your help to make it last."

"Okay. Thank you for trusting me. Let's talk about how I can help you."

Jim was so caring in how he helped me and the kids. He listened intently and gave suggestions on what he thought would be best, then he let me take my time to decide what to do. His insight was wise and clearly given with our best interests at heart. I knew I could trust him, and easily moved him into my "trusted wise counsel" category. He helped with more than just that one check and has earned my trust repeatedly.

More than sixteen years later, he's still taking care of us. He has walked me through a vehicle purchase, home purchases, job changes, retirement planning, and I could go on, but it would sound like an ad for his office. I mean, honestly, how many financial advisors can you call from the car dealership showroom floor and have them walk you through purchasing a new car to make sure you're getting the best deal? Jim has become more than just someone I respect immensely and trust implicitly: he has become a friend. I'll be forever indebted to him for playing such a key role in helping a lost widow find her bearings again.

And to think it started with obligatory attendance at what I thought was going to be a time-share-like presentation. Being introduced to Jim prior to Peter's passing was clear evidence that God did have a plan and I didn't need to worry.

CHAPTER 19

Promise #2

"Sell the boat. Fishing isn't your thing. There have been too many women who have tried to run their husband's boat after they were gone, and it hasn't worked out. They end up hiring a friend or family member who either takes advantage of the relationship or doesn't take care of the boat the way they should, and they go broke. A boat this size needs to be run by the owner. Nobody else will take pride or commit the level of responsibility required to make it work."

While this was a wise and appropriate route to take, it was a difficult task to accomplish. We'd grown a lot in our marriage through the process of starting and building the business. Just when we felt it was paying off, it ended. The memories attached to that boat were precious to me, and it felt as though I'd be selling those memories by selling it.

We'd spent so much time as a family on the *Miss Sarah*.

After our first summer with the boat, we started to have repeat customers who remembered the kids and some who even became friends. We worked hard, which was a gift we felt we were giving our kids as well. We wanted to show them a good work ethic and parents who worked together toward a common goal. It wasn't always fun, so they saw the difficult times as well, but that was okay because they saw us work through the struggles together.

As we worked on the boat, I'd recall a comment I frequently made in high school that I'd never marry a commercial fisherman. The lifestyle of an absent husband and father wasn't appealing to me. *Ha! Look at me now. Not only am I married to a fisherman, but we own our own boat.* I loved it, though, and was proud of Peter and how hard he worked. The boat was our livelihood, and it became our home away from home. The memories made during those days were precious and I wouldn't trade them for anything. I'm thankful for those years.

That's why it tore me apart to think about selling the *Miss Sarah.* But Peter had been very clear about it, and I'd made a promise. The boat was Peter's dream, and I'd just done what I needed to do to make sure his dream came true.

There was a moment when it became a challenge to keep my promise though. A little over a month after Peter passed, his cousin inquired about leasing it, and I almost caved. I had a visit from his cousin's girlfriend who wanted to talk to me about leasing the boat. Emotions were still raw, and I knew it was difficult for him to come and ask me himself. His girlfriend (he might not have known he was going to marry her at that point, but I did) was strong enough to have the conversation with me on his behalf. As she presented the business proposition, I had a moment where my heart leaped out in front of my brain and I almost exclaimed, "Yes, let's do this!" But my brain took control before I opened my mouth. I heard a small whisper in my ear reminding me that I'd made a promise. It was gut wrenching, but I let her know as gently as I could that I couldn't agree to the proposition. I couldn't lease it. I had to sell the boat.

The last thing I was willing to do was break a promise I'd made to Peter when I'd never have the opportunity to discuss with him why. If he were there, he might have told me to do it because it was his cousin, but I didn't know that for sure and my heart wouldn't let me go back on my word to him no matter who was standing in front of me. It broke my heart to say no. When she left I was tormented with a tornado of emotions. Guilt, sadness, and anger swirled inside me and threatened to tear apart the small piece of me that was still intact. I wanted so badly to do this for them, but couldn't.

I knew what it would have meant to them and what it would have meant to me and the kids for Peter's cousin to have the *Miss Sarah.* I also knew that the conversation Peter had had with me the night before he died was a gift because it freed me from playing the what-if game for the rest of my life. If I'd gone back on my promise, I'd have run that what-if question through my mind for the rest of my days. Maybe that was a selfish move, but it's what I believed I had to do. Even though my heart still hurts over that decision, I don't question it.

I listed the boat for sale through a broker within a couple of months of Peter's passing, and a year later finally received a call from him: "Stephanie, I have a buyer." All at once I was relieved and heartbroken.

"Do I know who it is? Can you tell me the buyer's name?" He told me the buyer's name and I could feel the tears well up in my eyes. I knew him and was thankful. His mom had been Peter's kindergarten teacher. She was one of the loveliest ladies I knew, and it brought great joy and relief to know her son was going to own our boat.

It took quite some time to get the paperwork together, but the day I met the buyer at the bank to sign all the final papers is embedded in my heart forever. I sat in the dark leather chair with the loan officer sitting across from me and the buyer sitting to my right. I knew I had to ask him one favor and my heart was racing as I gathered my courage. I couldn't look him in the eyes because I didn't think I'd be able to keep my composure if he turned down my request.

"Will you do me one favor please?" I whispered. He turned to me. "Will you please keep the name of the boat as it is? Please don't change it." With great kindness in his voice, he agreed wholeheartedly to not change the name. In that moment I felt all the gratitude and sorrow one could imagine. I was grateful for his response and yet was shattered knowing someone else now owned our *Miss Sarah*.

My thank-you was scarcely audible and I used all my strength to not fall to pieces in the office. A few rogue tears made their way down my cheeks as a box of tissues was quietly slid toward me from across the desk.

I left the bank and headed to the cemetery to tell Peter I'd kept my promise and sold the boat. I let the tears fall as I reconciled myself to the fact that a very beautiful chapter in my life had ended.

CHAPTER 20

Firsts

After losing a loved one, the milestones and significant anniversaries can at times feel like insurmountable events. When you know a "first" is coming up, it's almost impossible to not think about it and anticipate what you might feel when the day/time arrives. The first birthday they miss. The first anniversary you celebrate solo. The first vacation or holiday without them. I'd build each event up in my head and give myself a pep talk in preparation: *Okay, Stephanie, you can do this. You know this is a first and it won't be the last. You've survived the loss, so you can survive this too. You'll feel sad or hurt or angry, and that's okay. You can work through the feelings. You can do this! You can do this . . . I don't think I can do this.* Pretty much the same conversation with every milestone moment.

The first big milestone was our son's eighth birthday, which was less than two months after Peter's death. I can't even remember what I did for him on his special day if I did anything at all. I was still so numb at that time, I was just going through the motions. My poor boy who'd just experienced one of the greatest losses needed to be celebrated and his mom couldn't pull herself together enough to make him feel special. I remember feeling angry at Peter as I felt sorrow for my son and there was nothing I could do to make it better. That first milestone was a bust.

Many of the firsts following the birthday were a blur. I remember as each one drew closer, I'd get myself worked up. I'd give myself that great but epically ineffective pep talk, and would trudge through and barely make it.

Firsts

I anticipated that fall would be difficult because Peter was an avid hunter and we had great memories of that time of year. When I refer to him as an avid hunter, what I mean is that when he wasn't fishing for a profession, he was hunting, talking about hunting, or dreaming about hunting. It was his life. His identity. Yes, he was a commercial fisherman and a husband and father, but at his core he was a hunter, and was good at it. Fall was his season. Bear, deer, elk—you name it, he hunted it. It nearly took an act of God to get him out of the woods when he wasn't working. It was something I knew well about him before we even started dating, and it only bothered me when hunting came before installing a kitchen sink or fixing the plumbing under the house or my having the flu and trying to care for two kids. A glass of orange juice by the bed and a kiss goodbye just weren't sufficient, and we had many conversations about priorities during those years. If you're married to an avid hunter, you have my empathy. I get it and I stand with you in solidarity.

That first fall I was reminded of all the times I'd joke about being a "hunting widow" because of how often Peter would be gone. Then I found myself standing there as a real widow and didn't know how to approach it. I needed a distraction, which would be difficult because Perry was old enough that the hunting bug had fully rubbed off on him. I needed to make sure he was getting his time in the woods because I knew deep down that made him feel close to his dad. I was incredibly thankful for Peter's friends, who stepped up and offered to take Perry hunting with them. He needed that and I was relieved they could fill that gap for him because I certainly couldn't.

I thought I could be a hunter once. In fact, I emphatically insisted on being a hunter and Peter was more than happy to oblige. He bought me my own rifle, got me outfitted with all the appropriate gear and licensing, and took me hunting. We hunted together occasionally for a couple of years, but I wasn't very successful. Partly because I don't think he wanted me to take a trophy out from under him, and that was okay. I understood. Then the fall after our Perry was born, we hiked out in the woods and came upon a spike deer. It wasn't a trophy, but I was excited because I felt like I was contributing by putting meat in our freezer. I took my aim, and that deer went down with one shot. After crossing the hillside to where it had dropped, Peter turned and took one look at my face and said, "Hike back to the truck. I'll take care of this." As I turned away, he stopped me. "You aren't ever going to hunt with me again, are you?" I shook my head as I held back the tears.

The first fall without him was going to be tough, with our routine being turned upside down. The days of preparing food for hunting camp, getting up early to visit with him before he left in the morning, and having dinner ready or a bath run on the cold rainy days were gone. I wasn't sure how I was supposed to navigate this season, so planned a trip and had some of my LULAS go with me.

Something Peter and I had enjoyed doing together was watching professional bull riding. We each had our favorite riders and bulls and faithfully watched our top picks rise and fall throughout the season. I decided a way for me to reset my fall season pattern and celebrate Peter was to attend Professional Bull Riding Nationals in Las Vegas with my girlfriends. It was just what I needed.

The best part of the trip for me was watching Peter's favorite bull, Pandora's Box, and my favorite rider, Adriano Morães, during the finals. When one of those two took to the dirt, I stood and cheered as though I were pulling Peter's enthusiasm down from heaven and into that space. It was an amazing experience that helped a small part of me heal. Both bull and rider gave a show I felt was just for me and I'm still thankful for that memory.

The bonus was being in Vegas around masses of people who didn't know me or what I'd been through. It was a throng of enthusiastic people just enjoying life. I love people watching, and Vegas provided ample opportunity for me to observe and contemplate what goes on in some people's minds.

I returned home feeling refreshed and ready to be purposeful in how I moved forward with my life as well as with the kids. The trip allowed me to temporarily forget my responsibilities and just have some fun. Not in an irresponsible, throw-caution-to-the-wind kind of way, but in a release-from-the-feeling-of-heaviness kind of way. I could just laugh and enjoy life for a moment. It was rejuvenating. Even though we'd stayed up late and kept ourselves busy during the day, I felt rested and ready to take on life again.

Part of that refreshing was because my LULAS understood the purpose of the trip. They knew I needed to escape the reality of all the decision-making that had been my life for the previous six months and simply have some fun. They understood I needed to not feel any responsibility for myself or anyone else and just live in the moment, soaking up some of the craziness Vegas had to offer. They became my conscience, allowing me the freedom to not make decisions, giving my weary mind a break.

◄○►

The anniversary of the death of someone you love and cherish can be difficult to navigate. The anniversary of the day they passed can be the most painful event that brings the most apprehension and anxiety. Especially if they passed unexpectedly. It's difficult to process emotions during the trauma of the day, so sometimes all those emotions will start to surface in the days leading up to the anniversary.

We'd already been through birthdays and holidays and had learned to get through them better after each one we experienced. However, the anniversary of Peter's passing, which fell on the same day of our wedding anniversary, caused me to wonder how I should approach it.

I started getting anxious about the anniversary date of Peter's passing several months in advance. How would I honor Peter without falling apart again and losing all the ground I'd gained in counseling? Should I do something big, or just gloss over it? What if I chose to do something big and the kids felt like I'd opened old wounds and they didn't know how to respond? What if I didn't do anything and the kids felt like I'd forgotten their dad or not honored their need to do something to remember him on that day? Did they even know what date it was?

I decided to ask them that question. I asked them if they knew the date their dad had passed away and if they knew it was coming up soon. Their response? "Yes, it's your wedding day." I was floored. I struggled to conceal my shock. When I asked them how they remembered our wedding date, they said, "It's written on the painting that hangs on the dining room wall." Huh. Well, there you have it. As I looked at the sweet picture inscribed with "Peter & Stephanie Graham, April 19, 1997" written on it, I realized I'd done it once again—I'd underestimated my kids and their ability to see what was going on around them. Good job, Mom. Good job.

At that moment, I decided we needed to do something on the anniversary date to honor Peter. But again, how would we do this?

I was visiting with Malynnda and shared my dilemma with her: "What do you think I should do? I don't want it to be too much, but I don't want to gloss over it either. My instinct is to stuff the feelings down as deep as I can, ignore any inkling of emotion and just move on, but I'm trying not to pass my bad habits on to my kids. So, what do you think?" Her reply was so quick and simple that I knew it was exactly what we needed to do.

"Well, when he died, he got a new life in heaven, so why don't you celebrate his first birthday in heaven with Jesus?"

My jaw dropped and tears welled up in my eyes. I could picture it. A beautiful scene of the best party in heaven for his first birthday with Jesus. Oh, my goodness, what a vision! And something I knew my kids would understand. "That's it. That's perfect. Thank you so much for helping me with this."

She responded casually with a shrug of her shoulder: "It just popped into my head. There may be better options out there. It's just a thought."

There might have been other options, but this was the one I was rolling with.

I knew exactly what we were going to do. I'd taken that day off in anticipation of not being able to cope. I took the kids to the bakery, and they picked out a birthday cake with a grassy, outdoor scene on it. Perry had found a little figurine of a moose inside an outhouse, so he grabbed that to put on the cake and leave at the cemetery. We had the baker add "Happy Birthday Daddy" to the cake, grabbed some flowers and balloons, and set off to the cemetery for the birthday party. We tied the balloons to the vase on Peter's headstone and added the flowers and water. We contemplated what his birthday in heaven might be like, then cleaned up around his headstone and his cousin Jason's headstone (I always shared flowers with our dear Jason when I visited). We had some cake and juice, and after a bit the kids decided they were ready to go.

I think my friend had a genius idea. It helped to take what could have been a very solemn day and turn it into a celebration of Peter's life on earth as well as his new life in heaven. The kids didn't want to do this every year, and I was perfectly okay with that as long as they knew we could.

CHAPTER 21

Promise #3

"Stephanie, I want you to get remarried. I don't want you to be alone, and my kids deserve to have a dad."

I'll never forget the heaviness in the air when Peter relayed this promise to me. These weren't just casual words or hopeful wishes coming from his mouth. He was speaking his heart and imploring me with almost desperation to give him the peace of knowing if something happened to him I'd make sure his family was taken care of in the ways he needed them to be taken care of but wouldn't be able to do himself.

I'd slowly been trying to figure out how to keep this promise I'd made to Peter, as it felt like the most difficult, and almost unbearable, one to consider. This promise Peter had asked—no, more like flat-out held me hostage and demanded I promise him before he'd let me out of the car—felt more like a betrayal than a promise. At the time I had all but crossed my fingers behind my back, like a child swearing they didn't take a cookie without permission or promising your friend that if they jump in the lake, you'll follow. *Just kidding! I had my fingers crossed, so I don't have to do it.*

I didn't want to do it. I didn't want to make this promise because I didn't see how I could ever keep it. How could I possibly ever love anyone again in my life? I made the promise though. I looked him in the eyes and promised him that if something were to happen to him, I'd remarry and make sure his kids had a dad. I agreed they deserved that. I, on the other hand, would be perfectly capable of living by myself. Peter knew me well enough to know that if he didn't make me promise, I wouldn't do it.

I was reminded this promise was in truth a gift. I was given a dream that horrified me, triggering a conversation with Peter that settled all the "what ifs" or "would he have wanted" questions. I know widows and widowers who have played the "what would they have wanted me to do" game and it's almost tortuous to watch them agonize over every simple decision. I was released from that and for someone who already suffers from decision-making paralysis, this was a God-given gift in extra measure!

To be honest, I thought anyone who could get remarried after losing their spouse must not have really, truly loved them in the first place. How could I think of moving forward with dating or even contemplate marriage after losing Peter? Would this mean I didn't really love him? Well, that was just ridiculous. He was my best friend. Yes, we had some difficult times and yes, I was really focusing on those difficult times after he was gone. It was easier to think of the hardships or the things I didn't particularly care for than to think about the good times. My grief was easier to manage if I remembered our troubles, his temper, the arguments. When I felt grief rising in me, I was able to stuff it back down by remembering the negative. That worked for me. For a time.

However, when I was being honest with myself and allowed my mind to remember the good times, I was able to realize that getting remarried would be a testament to the life we'd had together. If I'd experienced a truly horrible marriage, I wouldn't be willing to risk experiencing that again. If my marriage to Peter wasn't good, I know myself well enough to know that I'd have dug my heels in and said, *Promise or no promise, I'm not doing that again*. I'd have been willing to deal with whatever consequences might have come my way.

Our marriage was far from perfect, but it was successful. I've yet to meet a couple who have a perfect marriage. I'm talking about marriages where two people have labored together to make it work and in the end what you have is a beautiful picture of a successful marriage—that's something to be celebrated! Peter and I had a marriage we were laboring through at times, but were doing it together. I knew we'd done our best to be successful, and that was something worth honoring.

Keeping my promise to Peter and taking the risk of loving someone and allowing them to love me was the best way I could honor our marriage. When I surrendered to this thought and became willing to put my heart out there, I was stunned at how quickly love came my way.

CHAPTER 22

Dating for
the First Time

I didn't know how to approach the dating process. Dating wasn't something I had substantial experience of, but if Peter wanted me to remarry, I probably needed to date first. How did one meet someone when they had two young kids and worked full time? Thankfully, I didn't have to put too much effort into the process. About five months into my journey as a widow, I was approached by a kind gentleman who was brave enough to ask me if I'd go to dinner.

Our paths had crossed through work, but we didn't know each other more than on a first-name basis. He wasn't a "local," so didn't know Peter, which made it easier for me to accept his offer—it didn't feel like a pity date. He was genuinely interested in me. The nerves that accompanied me on that evening were apparent in my flushed cheeks, quivering voice, and sweaty hands. I enjoyed myself and we met a couple more times, but it was clear it wasn't going to evolve any further than friendly conversation, which I did appreciate.

I had a few failed dates after that, which I chalked up to "practice." It felt too soon to be dating, but I justified it by telling myself, *It's just dating. I'm not getting married. I'm just letting someone take me to dinner and engage in adult conversation.*

Don't Worry—I Have a Plan.

I prayed and prayed, asking God to either do the work for me or release me from it completely. I didn't enjoy dating. It was awkward and uncomfortable. I needed God to bring me the man He wanted me to be with, and I needed someone I could love because at that moment I didn't think it was possible for me to truly love again.

While visiting with Andrea one day, I expressed my apprehension mixed with my desire to move forward. I was in an awkward place: feeling as though I were supposed to mourn for the rest of my life but also acknowledging I was thirty years old and had a whole lifetime ahead of me. Truthfully, being alone for the next sixty-plus years didn't sound great to me, but getting married again didn't sound great either.

As I explained everything I was feeling, she pointed to my left hand.

"What?" I asked. "What's wrong with my hand?"

"Your ring."

"What about my ring?"

"You're still wearing it. One, are you truly ready to date while still wearing it, and two, maybe you should consider how a guy is going to feel about dating someone who is still wearing a wedding ring."

"Oh." This was the difficult reality of the crossroads where I sat. My heart physically ached at the thought of removing my ring. "Do I have to take it off?"

She shrugged. "Only you know that answer."

She left me to ponder what I was feeling. I knew she was right, but how could I remove my ring? I could move it to my right hand, but knew myself—having the visual reminder with me every day would prevent me from allowing someone else into my world.

I considered what else I could do other than removing it and putting it away but, in the end, knew I needed to take it off and tuck it away safely. This was painful but necessary. As I slowly removed it from my finger, I was reminded of my wedding vow "Till death do us part." I held my ring in my hand, the original symbol of Peter's promise to love me for forever, and let the tears fall. Then I carefully wrapped it in a silk pouch, tucked it lovingly into the jewelry box my grandfather had made for me, closed the lid, and mourned the symbolic burial of our marriage. *I kept my promise to Peter the day we got married. I'll keep my promise to him now.*

◄○►

I confided in my dad one day that I'd gone on a couple of dates and had felt super uncomfortable. Not necessarily because of the guys—well, one guy was uncomfortable—but mostly because I didn't know how to proceed. Dad was surprised to hear I was ready to date. It had only been six months, but then he encouraged me to step out of the norm for dating: "Stephanie, I have a coworker who signed up for an online dating service. From what this person tells me, it's done well, and they felt safe throughout the process. Why don't you look into that?"

I did some research and decided signing up might be a good option. I could just try it. Online dating?! Kind of, but not in the way most people think of it these days. At least I didn't feel it was quite the same. Especially after completing a full online personality test. That was a lot of work! It took me three days to complete it because I spent so much time overthinking every question and making sure I was answering with 100 percent honesty.

After finally completing the process, it had me narrow down my options like I was online shopping for a new car:

What geographic range would you prefer for dating? Any. I wasn't going to put limits on this.

What's the age range of a person you're willing to date? My age and ten years older, I guess?

Will you consider someone who has been divorced? Yes.

How about widowed? It was a no to someone who was widowed. I was bringing enough baggage with me—I didn't want to double that load. (As if there's any person alive without baggage, but I didn't want as much as I felt I had at the time.)

Don't Worry—I Have a Plan.

Kids or no kids? No kids. My kids and I had been through a lot, and I didn't want them to feel like they had to compete for attention. It wouldn't be fair for either side.

After narrowing down the rest of my "wish list," I uploaded a picture for my profile. I chose one of me wearing my red baseball cap and hugging my dog. I figured they didn't need to see any more of me than my face, and knowing I was a dog person might help them decide quickly if they were interested. Some people just aren't dog people and that's okay, but not when my dog was a part of the package deal. I said a prayer and hit "Submit."

Then came the waiting. And worrying. And doubting the decision to do online dating.

The process, while arduous, was done well and made me feel safe with nothing more than my first name and some vague and basic information available to others on the platform. I didn't feel there was a threat of someone unexpectedly showing up to meet me because there was no way of knowing where I lived. Internet searches were not as easy then as they are now.

I had my own list of characteristics I thought I'd want in a partner and, as I pondered my wish list, recorded them in my journal. It wasn't a long list, but it included the things most important to me in that moment. *I'd like someone who has a strong relationship with God. Someone who is patient and kind, will love my babies as his own, and will love me even when I think about Peter and miss him.*

After a week or two and a few conversations, a match named Derek popped up on my list. His picture and profile piqued my interest. He was an educator who lived about three hours away. Divorced with no kids and a kind, genuine smile. I spent a couple of days praying and contemplating whether I wanted to reach out to this one or not and, ultimately, decided to go for it. Why not? We were only communicating through an app, right?

For a month we used the website's secure messaging to communicate before I finally gave him my personal email address and eventually my phone number. We spent weeks talking on the phone for hours each night and sending emails back and forth occasionally throughout the day. We talked about everything. No topic was off-limits. We found our childhoods were similar, with both of us being raised in Christian homes by strict, conservative parents, and we each had one set of grandparents who lived close by. We talked openly about our previous marriages and how we'd contributed positively and negatively to them and what we'd want to do differently if given the opportunity.

I was very earnest in describing the hurt and grief I was still feeling and believed I'd always feel. I wanted to make sure he understood this would always be a part of me and would play a part in my future decision-making. I was transparent that my kids were my everything. "Since they lost their dad, it's my responsibility to give them what they need. Anybody who dates or maybe someday marries me needs to understand that."

Derek was honest about his past marriage and the role he'd played in its not being successful. He shared the disappointment he felt in himself and how he was continuing to work on being a better person and hopefully a better husband to someone in the future.

After a while, he approached the subject of meeting in person, and I froze. I wanted to, but was also apprehensive. I was comfortable talking on the phone for now, so put it off, feeling hesitant to take the next step. I needed to make sure I was being very careful with this process. I had a habit of letting what other people might think or say influence my decision-making, and others' comments were contributing to my hesitation. People felt I wasn't giving myself adequate time to mourn, and they didn't think the timing was appropriate.

Something a lot of people don't see or understand is that when you're the one who directly experienced the loss, you don't get a break from grieving or thinking about your lost loved one. Many of those who are even one degree removed from the situation, let alone two degrees or more, are given a break from thinking about the person who died. They have their normal lives they can engage in and only think of the loss when reminded. When you're the spouse or child, you don't get that break—the person is always on your mind. So, I felt I was ready to move toward this next step faster than those around me because I was forced to deal with my loss and grief every single waking hour, not just as if Peter happened to cross my mind a couple of times a week.

It was December and the kids and I were attending the first LULAS Christmas party. I shared with the LULAS that Derek had asked to meet in person and I was feeling hesitant. I didn't feel hesitant about meeting him, but was worried about what people would say and how this might affect the kids. I wanted their thoughts. I needed to make sure I was considering all possibilities and concerns.

The LULAS ran a list of questions my way. "Where would you meet? What will you do when you meet? What warning signs will you look for? Have you prayed about it?" After their thoughtful inquisition, they all agreed that we'd explored all possibilities, and it was solely my decision. Whatever I decided, they'd be supportive.

Malynnda had given each of us a yearlong devotional/journal for Christmas. Mine was bound with a beautiful lavender leather-like material with the words "A Gentle Spirit" embossed on the cover. I don't know if she considered me a gentle spirit or believed I needed to be more like a gentle spirit but, either way, I loved it and couldn't wait to start journaling in it. I opened it to the date and read the printed scripture aloud. It was Revelation 3:8, "I know your deeds. See, I've placed before you an open door that no one can shut. I know that you have little strength, yet you have kept my word and have not denied my name."

Now, I don't believe that everything we experience or come across is a sign or that you can pluck a scripture from the Bible and make it relevant to your situation, but this felt like a very pointed message to me. An open door. And it made me ask, "God, was this part of your plan when you told me not to worry?" I needed to take this opportunity and see what would happen. Maybe it wasn't what God had in store but, then again, maybe it would be exactly the gift He'd planned for my life. I wouldn't know if I didn't take a step forward.

I sent a text to Derek asking if he could meet that evening. We decided to meet at a popular restaurant centrally located between our homes. I had each of my friends agree to text or call me at different times to check on me, and we agreed on a code word in case things weren't going well and I needed assistance in exiting. Interestingly, I wasn't very nervous—an odd sensation for me, because I've always been apprehensive and shy around new people. But meeting Derek didn't seem to scare me. Maybe our hours of conversation each day had allowed me to feel a level of familiarity and comfort with him. This made me believe I needed to be even more cautious so I wasn't caught off guard.

I arrived early and waited in the restaurant parking lot. I wanted to be there first to watch him drive up. That gave me the advantage of verifying how he'd described his car and himself. I had only one picture of him to reference, so if his picture and car description didn't match what I saw in person, I'd be able to drive away and not look back.

I didn't have to wait long before I saw his silver sports car roll up next to me. It was exactly as he described and when he stepped out, I realized he didn't look exactly like his picture. He was handsomer and more relaxed looking than his picture. This was a very good start to our meeting.

While he looked comfortable, I sensed he was just as nervous as I was as he reached out for a handshake. "Hi. I'm Derek."

We shook hands awkwardly like we were making introductions at a business meeting.

"Hi Derek. I'm Stephanie. It's nice to meet you in person." I don't think either of us was an expert at this first-meeting thing.

"It's pretty cold out here. Should we go in?" He motioned toward the restaurant. Eager to get inside, where it was warm, we walked to the entrance. He opened the door for me like a gentleman and checked in with the hostess. I was thankful she sat us closer to the entrance. Even though the wind rushed through whenever the door opened, I felt more comfortable away from a back table or booth. I didn't feel unsafe with Derek at all, but the overthinking, hypervigilant side of my brain was in control, and I needed to see the exit.

I was pleased when this gentleman not only opened the door for me but pulled my chair out from the table for me to sit on, let me order first and for myself, and paid for the meal even though I offered to split it.

Chivalry wasn't dead! I felt appreciation for the man who'd taught him how to treat a lady properly.

Throughout dinner we recapped all the conversations we'd had over the phone, confirming details as if to verify the validity of each other's stories. We found that everything was accurate and there were no surprises, which was a relief to me. I knew people could tell a good story about themselves, but in person the fake persona wore off. We kept our conversation mostly at the surface level and dipped into deep topics only occasionally. Something in his demeanor and the way he earnestly listened to me was comforting, and I felt a part of my heart I thought was dead start to beat again.

As we finished our dinner, he asked if I wanted to walk around the town or if I wanted to call it a night and we could head our separate ways. I'd really enjoyed our conversation, but mostly I liked how I felt just being with him, so I chose to walk around town for a bit. Walking around sounded like a great idea, but it didn't last long. There just isn't much to look at in a small town at six o'clock on a Sunday evening, so we headed to a coffee shop, grabbed a cup, and visited a little while longer. I enjoyed the conversation with Derek and felt perfectly at ease with him.

There wasn't any one thing that particularly stood out or anything he said that made a significant difference for me, but just being with him made me feel like we'd known each other our entire lives. I didn't feel like I was meeting him for the first time and I'm sure all the phone conversations helped with that, but what I was feeling was different. What I was feeling was a familiarity like I was being reunited with someone I'd always known.

All evening, I knew we were constantly surrounded by people, but was almost unaware of anyone around us. It felt like it was just the two of us and nobody else existed.

I could have spent the entire night just being with him, sharing stories and thoughts and dreams, but my responsibilities drew me back to reality. "It's starting to get late, and I need to go pick up my kids."

"Of course. Can I call you later?"

"Yes. I really enjoyed my evening. Thank you for driving all this way to have dinner."

"I really enjoyed myself," he said as he stuck out his hand to shake mine. I looked at him with a bit of confusion. A handshake felt formal and a little insulting, yet was a hug too forward? A kiss was definitely out of the question for me on a first date. He sensed what I was thinking and asked if he could hug me.

Ooh, I'll take a hug. "Yes, a hug would be nice," I said with a smile.

I'm not going to lie when I say it was a bit strange hugging someone new. My heart was savoring every bit of affection and wanted the hug to last longer, but my brain wasn't allowing my emotions to run the show. My desire to hop in his car and take off with him was thwarted by my logical thinking and a begrudging reminder to not rush into anything. I took a step back. "Thank you again. You'll call me later?"

He smiled as he realized I wanted to continue talking after meeting him in person. "I'll call you later. Drive safe."

We got in our cars and headed to the interstate on-ramps. I took the north ramp and he took the south. When I got onto the interstate, I called Malynnda, who was watching the kids, to let her know I was on my way. She asked me how it had gone and, without skipping a beat, I said, "I think I'm going to marry him."

"Well, okay then," she said. "The kids were good tonight."

CHAPTER 23

———

Taking Things Slow

I found out months later that as Derek was taking the south on-ramp, he'd called a friend and told him he was going to marry me. I guess when you know, you know.

We talked on the phone later that night and Derek asked when he could see me again. "Do you like driving around and looking at Christmas lights?"

Christmas is one of my favorite holidays. "Yes, I love driving around looking at lights!" I answered emphatically. He offered to drive up in a few days to look at Christmas lights one evening. So, we made plans to meet in a neighboring town, keeping the kids at what I felt was a safe distance. I felt the butterflies in my stomach and was excited they were still alive. I thought for sure they'd withered away when Peter died. *Welcome back, old friends.*

We met at a coffee shop, and he surprised me with a large bouquet of beautiful flowers. I was slightly surprised that I felt no hesitation as I got in his little silver sports car. He drove us around the local neighborhoods, and we marveled at the festive lights while talking nonstop. Christmas lights give everything a magical glow and made our evening feel enchanting. I felt at ease with Derek, so when he asked if he could hold my hand, I didn't hesitate for a moment. I felt that zing of electricity run through me and a wave of excitement that this small gesture stirred so much emotion.

We decided to stop by my friend Tina's house while driving around. I thought I'd do a little test run with a friend to see how they'd respond to seeing me with someone and what they'd think of Derek. I wasn't so naive as to think I didn't need someone else to test for a hidden "creep" factor. Tina wasn't home, but her husband was. After we visited for a while, he looked over at me, winked, and gave me a quick thumbs-up. I was taking it. I mean, this man chose one of my best friends to be his wife, so his opinion was pretty solid in my eyes.

I knew at some point I'd need to introduce him to the kids, but wanted to be careful in how I did that. I wanted to protect them and make sure I didn't introduce them to someone who wouldn't be in their lives long-term. Perry and Sarah didn't need the interruption and I didn't need to create any situations where they'd be let down. It was almost a month after Derek and I had met for the first time in person before we talked about his meeting the kids. He was respectful of my wishes and told me to let him know when I was ready.

Whenever we'd talk about kids and discuss how much work parenting is, he'd do his best to convince me he understood about parenting and the work involved in this most important role. He adamantly believed that because he was a schoolteacher, he could easily be a parent too.

Isn't that cute.

While I have much respect for teachers and what they do, I truly believe that teaching and parenting are two different jobs. They may be equally exhausting, but are opposite in managing. I tried to help him understand that having students in your care for six hours a day wasn't the same as having them in your home 24/7 with no summer or winter breaks. He kept insisting that he understood, and every time I'd chuckle and say, "Okay . . ."

I reminded him regularly that if we moved forward together, the kids and I would be dragging a lot of baggage and a dog with us, and we'd very likely experience some rough times in the future. He assured me he understood and was prepared for what might come our way. I think this is when I realized he might be a "learn by experience" kind of guy. *Buckle up, buddy, things are going to get bumpy.*

Don't Worry—I Have a Plan.

We agreed that it would be challenging and we'd need to work together moving forward. Both of us believed we were headed toward marriage, but neither of us was brave enough to say the words yet.

I'd decided to tell the kids about Derek during our upcoming trip to Disneyland. I knew we'd have the freedom to speak openly without others' influence, and how could they be upset when we'd be in the happiest place on earth? Right? I hoped.

◄○►

We were about to encounter our first Christmas without Peter and I was unsure how I'd make the holiday special for the kids. Christmas and Easter have always been my two favorite holidays, and I didn't know how to approach this first one. *Do I just move forward with decorations, the tree, presents, and a big meal with family, or do I plan something small with just me and the kids? Or . . . do I take the kids and run away?*

Run away. That's what I decided to do. If I stayed home and tried to do something small, I'd end up offending family members who wanted to be with the kids. I also didn't want the kids to spend Christmas surrounded by sad people watching them for signs of grief or projecting their own grief onto them. We needed to make some happy memories, so I decided to take them to the happiest place on earth. I got on the phone and booked Christmas in Disneyland.

I wanted to make the trip as positive as I could. Even though we wouldn't be home, we'd still have Christmas. I purchased, wrapped, and shipped their presents to the hotel ahead of our arrival, and the staff there were so helpful by hiding their gifts in the closet of our room the morning we arrived. I splurged by renting a town car to pick us up and take us to the airport (that was more for me than for the kids). We were the perfect mixture of apprehension and excitement as we set out, determined to make it a great experience.

It might not have been the traditional Christmas we'd always had in the past, but we enjoyed ourselves. Being on vacation by myself with my kids made me feel like we'd accomplished something significant. It proved to me we could be happy with just the three of us if that ended up

- 150 -

being our situation. I gained confidence in myself as their mom, and we created a tighter bond with each other in the process. That trip allowed for healing to occur where we hadn't expected it.

Taking the kids to Disneyland was my attempt to protect them from a sad first Christmas without their dad, so I did hesitate to tell them about Derek. I wondered if they'd resent the timing. I prayed and asked my LULAS to pray about timing, and when the kids and I arrived at our hotel in Disneyland, I felt the timing was right. The first thing we did after unpacking was head to the hotel restaurant and order some lunch. We were starving and I was nervous. Maybe telling them over lunch would be good. If they got upset, we could head to Disneyland and get happy.

About the time our french fries arrived, I was ready to talk to them. I took a deep breath and said a little prayer. As they loaded their plates with hot fries and ketchup, I said, "I have something to tell you."

They looked at me with expectant eyes.

"Your daddy didn't want us to be alone after he was gone. He wanted me to find someone who could love us and be part of our family."

Whoa, this was harder than I thought it would be. I swallowed my tears. "We can never ever replace your daddy, and I'd never want to do that, but he also said we deserved to have someone in our lives to love us."

I searched their faces and they seemed to be tracking with what I was telling them. I took a moment to breathe down the tears that kept surfacing. They each grabbed a fry and while Perry dipped his in ketchup, Sarah used hers to scoop up the ketchup, leaving a smear across her plate. Happy tastebuds, happy children? *Let's do this.*

I watched their faces and tried to predict what they were thinking. I explained that I'd been talking to someone very nice, I thought they'd like him, and wanted them to meet him. "How do you feel about this?" I eased back in my seat and held my breath as I waited for an explosion of tears and anger.

Neither one of them moved for a moment. They just sat quietly examining their plates while I dangled on the edge of panic and anxiety. My girl was staring at her plate of ketchup scattered with a few fries, scowling and clearly not happy. *Oh boy, this could go very badly.* She was expressing her unhappiness well through her expressive face, so I continued to wait and give her time. When I turned to my son and asked him what he was thinking, his words became the calm that washed over his sister. With his eyes brimming with tears, he confidently told me, "I've been praying for this, Mom. I'm happy about it." My heart was overjoyed to see that I didn't just crush him more, and felt my own tears rise to the surface. I looked at my daughter and saw her studying her brother, then she looked at me cautiously: "Yeah, me too," she said, as she returned her attention to her food and took another bite of her ketchup-drenched french fry.

I knew they didn't fully understand all this meant or what might happen next. Heck, *I* didn't fully understand all of it but, for that moment, I was able to share with them what they needed to know, and we were all in agreement that it was a good thing. They spent the time we stood waiting in lines at Disneyland to quiz me about him. They wanted to know everything they could about who he was and what he did. On Christmas day, we spent our time in the hotel opening gifts and ordering room service. The questions kept coming, so I offered to let them talk to Derek on the phone. The conversation was brief and revolved around telling him what they got for Christmas, but I think allowing them to hear his voice helped to make him feel real to them.

Disneyland was jam-packed with people, and despite our sharing our vacation with what felt like half the world's population, our time there was special. I was thankful I'd made the decision to take them out of town by myself for Christmas and so thankful for the amazing memories we made along the way. Thinking of our first vacation and Christmas without Peter makes my heart feel the warmth of the love shared among the three of us during that time.

◄○►

Returning home from our holiday trip, I was faced with the mixed emotions of anticipation and angst. Now that I'd talked to the kids about Derek and they'd each talked to him on the phone, it made sense for them to meet him, but was that really the right decision? It all felt so fast, and I didn't want my desire to keep my promises to Peter to be the driving force for my moving forward with Derek. I knew that would be the wrong groundwork when laying the foundation of a relationship.

I wanted to make sure we were moving forward for the right reasons and that I wasn't trying to "get over" my grief faster by diving into something new. I knew there were those who were concerned about this as well and I wanted to listen to them and what they were concerned about to make sure I wasn't being blind to anything. While that sounded great, it ended up being overwhelming. Hearing everyone else's opinions on what I should do really just confused things.

Even with my heart open to dating and the kids saying they were okay with my doing so, I was still hesitant to move forward in any serious relationship status. The kids seemed to get more excited about Derek as the days went by. On our way home from our trip, I messaged a dear friend and told her the kids seemed okay with my dating, but I just didn't know if I was making the right decision. I didn't think I could share my heart again. Partly because it didn't feel whole, so how could I be in a relationship with someone if I didn't have access to my entire heart?

Her response: "Stephanie, God has given you a gift. All you have to do is accept it."

She was right and I didn't need to hear anymore. So, I decided to stop seeking others' opinions and simply turn to what I knew was my best resource for guidance. I prayed and asked God for direction and discernment. He was the only one who knew the plan for my life, and I needed to rely on His guidance.

A few days before the New Year, I received a visit from a longtime friend who'd come home to visit her parents. She was asking me how I was doing, and I shared that I was dating someone I felt very serious about. "I do worry about stepparent dynamics should this progress the way I see it going. I need to make sure the kids are loved and cared for."

She reminded me her dad was a stepdad, which I'd forgotten. He was the only dad I'd ever known her to have. He'd come into her life at around the same age Perry was at the time. Then she said something that sank deep and left me dropping my doubt to the floor. "Stephanie, not everybody is lucky enough to have their own children, and there are a lot of kids who need someone to step in and be their parent. The world needs more people willing to be good stepparents. It sounds to me like Derek is willing to be that."

She was right and my kids were in the group of those needing a good stepparent. *Okay, God. Is this the message you've sent me?* I felt this conversation with my friend didn't happen by chance and Peter was right—our kids deserved to have a dad.

CHAPTER 24

Marriage 2.0

Deciding to marry again wasn't easy. It would mean another major event and change in our lives, and I needed to be certain about Derek before initiating more of that change. Our physical distance made it easier for us to have good conversations without interruption. Spending three to four hours a night talking on the phone allows you to really get to know a person—and the more time we spent talking, the more the doubts fell away.

Derek was kind and understanding of what I'd been through. Meeting him and getting to know him felt like an incredible gift in itself, and the more time I spent with him, the more I felt grounded and calmer. In a time when I was doing my best to just make it one day at a time, struggling to see what was up and what was down, he helped bring my world from spinning to a place of peace and momentary control. I'm not saying I was always in control or always made the best decisions, but Derek brought a calmness for me that allowed my whirlwind thoughts to slow and become steady instead of continuing at the frantic pace in which they'd been moving.

Knowing we were both coming from places of hurt from previous relationships and acknowledging how our relationship would affect the kids, we became purposeful in our conversations about our future. I didn't want to pretend we were in a better place than we truly were, and he didn't want to minimize our experience by pushing himself into our lives. We acknowledged our need to allow room for error and grace because we were certain we'd mess things up from time to time—we are, after all, human. So, we committed to keeping God at the center of our relationship, praying together, and separately seeking guidance on our next steps.

Every day we spent physically apart from each other felt like a week. We did our best to spend every weekend together. During one of our visits Derek turned to me and said, "I hope this isn't too fast, but I want you to know that after meeting you for dinner that first time, I told my friend I knew I wanted to marry you."

Ummm . . . do I tell him I felt the same? Is that weird, coincidental, or kismet? Just go for it.

"Really? That's very interesting, because while you were telling your friend that, I was saying the same thing to Malynnda."

He got a little twinkle in his eye and, a month later, while the kids and I were visiting him, he presented me with a beautiful ring and asked me to marry him. I said yes.

I was both elated and scared. I was honored that this man wanted me to partner with him for life, willing to take on the brokenness I was bringing with me. It also meant, to be able to live life fully with Derek, I needed to fully accept all that had happened and all we'd lost.

A part of me wanted to stay locked into the moment and place before Peter left us. Feeling my heart being torn between two places made me question if my answer of yes to Derek was appropriate to give. Was it fair to Derek for me to commit to him when a part of my heart still belonged to Peter? People were asking if I'd completed the appropriate period of mourning, and I was asking myself if I were at a point considered proper to remarry. Then I asked myself, *Why am I letting others' opinions of an appropriate mourning period dictate my future?*

My friend's words rang in my ears: "Stephanie, God has given you a gift. All you have to do is accept it."

She was right. I'd spent every day praying and seeking God's guidance and trusting the promise He'd given me. I'd asked Him to show me the plan He had for me and to bring me the people He'd chosen to be in my life. When I allowed doubt to creep in or I allowed other people to speak their doubt to me, I risked missing the blessing God had for me. So, I prayed and waited and listened.

Living 175 miles apart meant Derek and I saw each other on weekends and sometimes midweek when he was up for a long night. During one of our weekend visits, Derek shared with me that he'd been spending time praying over our relationship and future.

"Stephanie, I went for a drive the other day. It was a beautiful day, so I drove the Historic Columbia River Highway and ended up parking at Vista House. The view was beautiful, and I sat there and prayed for us. I also prayed that one day, when I get to heaven, I'll get to meet Peter and he'll thank me for being a good husband to you and a good father to his kids. That's my prayer. That I'll honor him and his family by being everything you and the kids need."

With tears stinging my eyes, I said, "You really prayed that? Do you really wish for that?"

"Yes, I do. I don't want to let you, the kids, or him down."

"Wow, I don't know how to respond other than to say thank you for wanting that for us."

And we lived happily ever after.

Kidding!

As you can imagine there's a lot that has to be done when getting married and moving a family to a new home, and each task that arose was met with what felt like a too-simple solution. I didn't want to sell my house, but didn't want to rent it to just anyone either. I needed to be able to trust whoever was living in it to take care of things because I wouldn't be just around the corner to respond to needs. With very little effort, I was connected with a young girl I knew who had been one of the kids' former babysitters who was looking for a place to rent. I loved her and knew she was trustworthy. Win!

I knew I wanted to continue working, so this meant embarking on the difficult and exhausting task of searching, applying, and interviewing for jobs in a town where I had no connections. I could have chosen to stay home but enjoyed working. I applied for several jobs I felt I was qualified for and within a week of applying at a local school district office had an interview scheduled. I had no school experience, other than being a student and parenting students, but this job would afford me the flexibility I wanted with the kids. I walked away from the interview feeling confident I'd failed. Before I got home, I'd been offered and had accepted a position that ended up being one of the best experiences of my life, connecting me with people I love dearly and hold in the highest regard.

It felt as though the path to marrying Derek had been laid out before me. Even though I couldn't see the entire pathway, as I took each step forward, a little more of the path was revealed, allowing me to move forward with confidence and peace knowing I was following God's plan.

◄o►

We got married in Derek's backyard on a blistering hot day in July with family and a few close friends in attendance. With Perry and Sarah by my side and a feeling of total confidence, I walked toward Derek to the sound of Sarah Kelly singing "Fall into You." I felt a deep connection with the lyrics as I felt my heart awaken to this new love I'd been given.

◄o►

Derek and I had had many long conversations before we got married regarding where we should live. He offered to find a job in the Westport area and relocate so the kids and I didn't have to move. I declined his generous offer and said the kids and I would move and, in doing so, I'd be keeping my promise to Peter. So, the kids and I left the only home we knew. I vacillated between excitement and sorrow as I packed up our home. It wasn't easy feeling like I was packing up our memories even though I knew moving was what we were supposed to do.

Telling Peter's parents that we'd be moving wasn't easy. When I was able to have that conversation with them, Patty had one request: "Please don't change their last name. Please keep it as Graham." She thought that my getting married and changing my last name meant I'd change the kids' last name to Derek's as well.

I was shocked by this request: "It had never occurred to me that changing their last name was an option. I guess if when they got older and wanted to, we'd discuss it, but there would be no reason at all to change it now. Patty, I won't be changing their last name, and if you're worried let me assure you that you guys are in our lives forever."

Derek and I had had multiple conversations about family dynamics and my desire to stay in contact with Patty and Daryl: "They lost their son; I won't take their grandchildren away from them. They're as close to me as my own parents, so they're a part of my life forever. This is an absolute deal breaker, so I need to know that you're going to be okay with this."

Derek fell in love with Patty and Daryl right away, so this wasn't an issue for him at all. My parents, Derek's parents, Patty and Daryl—we all melded together to make an amazing family of support. Yes, there were hiccups along the way, but that's to be expected when navigating a new family dynamic while also navigating grief. I know it wasn't easy for Patty and Daryl, and didn't expect it to be, but knew that, together, we could work through all of it. I just needed confirmation that we wouldn't lose our family while choosing to live forward.

CHAPTER 25

Living Forward

Living forward—that's what I call that period of my life. There were plenty of times throughout the years that I wondered if I'd rushed things with Derek and moving the kids. I knew it was the right thing, but I'm a professional overthinker—especially when it comes to my own decision-making skills. I knew I was fulfilling my promise to Peter. Plus, I was beyond happy and so in love. However, over the years I'd heard many people make comments about those who remarried soon after losing a spouse. They questioned the widow's true feelings for her spouse or doubted her state of mind and ability to make sound decisions. An unwritten-grief timeline is a very unfair expectation to put on someone who is choosing to accept the gift of love and live their life forward.

I'd read it was more typical for men to remarry quickly, but there seemed to be a longer grieving expectation for women. I sensed there was extra concern when I took steps to continue with life. Some call it "moving on," but I like to call it living forward. I don't feel the term *moving on* was appropriate for what I was doing. I wasn't ignoring or abandoning what had happened, as that would have been physically impossible to do. The grief struck too deep for me to ever dream of extracting it from my heart. So, I knew that waiting to heal from my grief before living forward meant I'd be stuck in the past forever.

I don't make quick decisions unless I believe the decision is 100 percent the right one to make, and marrying Derek was the right decision.

Living Forward

Hearing people question or criticize my choice to live my life forward didn't deter me, but it did hurt. It's easy to look at someone else's situation and think you know what's best for them based on what you see on the outside. I've done it myself, and 99 percent of the time I've been wrong. We can't know the plans God has for other people or even for us until He decides to reveal them. Living forward was what allowed me to receive the gifts God was giving me and live out what He'd planned all along.

CHAPTER 26

Stuffing

Despite how difficult it was emotionally, I was thankful to be moving away from Westport and to a new home with Derek and the kids. I didn't want to leave my hometown, but was thankful for the way God had orchestrated the move, allowing me to not only keep two of my promises to Peter but also start a new life with Derek.

It wasn't long before I realized what a relief it was not to be haunted by memories of Peter everywhere I turned. But what I saw as a positive in the break from constant heartache turned into a negative over time. I didn't realize that the constant reminders of Peter were actually helping me work through my grief. I thought the two mini-Peters living with me were reminders enough. Perry and Sarah were both so much like their dad in many ways, and were a daily reminder of what we'd lost. I thought I didn't need to have any other landmark reminders popping up when I went grocery shopping, or to the school, or whenever I craved a sandwich for lunch at Original House of Pizza.

Even with my two living reminders being in my space daily, I was able to change my focus from "Oh, these sweet little reminders of sadness" to "Okay, these two kids need as normal a childhood as possible." They deserved a mom who was focusing on the future, and Derek deserved a wife who wasn't living her life longing for or mourning over the past.

So, I took all my grief and as many memories as I could gather and stuffed them into a box wrapped in denial and ignorance, tied it with a pretty little bow of naiveté, and shoved it as far down into the depths of my soul as possible.

What I wasn't prepared for was that over time as I continued adding more memories and moments of grief to that pretty little box, it became too small to contain it all. The box began to deteriorate from all the times I'd opened it just enough to stuff more inside and then closed it up again.

For a while I decided the grief that made its reappearance needed to be squashed completely. *Maybe I could focus on a different emotion and I won't have to address the grief.* So, I chose anger. I'd already experienced anger within the first two months after losing Peter. That anger felt different though. With that anger, I wanted to punch something. I wanted to bring Peter back so I could beat the crap out of him and let him die again. I was so angry with him for leaving me and abandoning his children. The anger tried to consume me then, but I wouldn't let it. I found a brief outlet that allowed me to get it out. One evening I called a friend to come get the kids and found myself in the backyard moving our wood pile. I didn't just move it—I threw it. I took each piece of the nicely stacked wood and hurled them against the shed, taking satisfaction with each piece that loudly smashed against the siding and bounced across the yard. It took until the last piece before I allowed the tears to replace my screams of rage.

A couple of years later, I was feeling a different kind of anger. I was tired of feeling grief and it annoyed me knowing I'd never be free from it. Instead of in a healthy way working through what I was feeling, I decided to let the annoyance pair itself with anger. Somehow this gave me a sense of control. The anger invited back all the memories of the difficult times throughout our life together. All the times he'd left me to go fishing. All the times he'd chosen hunting over spending time with me. All the arguments when he cut me down with his words. I kept all these memories in my easy-to-reference file until I convinced myself I was thankful he was gone and I could live a new life without his temper and hurtful words. I was better off without him.

The trouble was, none of that was truly how I felt. But our minds are a powerful weapon, and my mind told lies to help keep the grief stuffed deep down.

Don't Worry—I Have a Plan.

Every significant milestone or event when I started to feel sadness that he wasn't with us, I'd create a story of how he'd have ruined it by his presence. Holidays, birthdays, school concerts, playoff games, graduations—you name it. If there was a significant event that would invite thoughts of "Peter would have loved this." Or "I wish he could see his kids' accomplishment." I'd take that sentimental opportunity and obliterate it with "If Peter were here, he'd be disruptive." Or "If he were here, he'd probably say something to incite an argument." Thinking of how he could have ruined the moment helped me keep stuffing and made it possible for me to not cause a scene with tears or emotions I didn't want to deal with.

Yet every day a little bit of that tidy emotional box overstuffed with my grief was breaking down. I could feel that beautiful ribbon of naïveté I'd so carefully wrapped around the box fraying at the ends, weakening and allowing little pieces of my past hurt to rise to the surface.

As the years went by, it became more and more difficult to manage the memories interrupting my thoughts, and my ability to maintain my emotional facade became nearly impossible.

It's only been in recent years, when I've allowed myself the time and space to acknowledge and feel each emotion, that I've realized my fear of feeling prevented me from truly healing. In a way I robbed myself and my family of years of being a healthier version of myself—one where I wasn't expending unnecessary energy stuffing down the grief I was afraid to feel.

I was afraid if I allowed myself to feel the sadness and depth of grief I was experiencing, I'd break. I wouldn't be able to be the mom or wife I needed to be, which, ironically, is exactly what happened. Not addressing my emotions in a healthy manner prevented me from being the mom and wife I was created to be.

My dear reader, please, for the sake of your own emotional health and for those who need you, if you're stuffing down your emotions, please stop. Stop stuffing and start feeling. Find someone to help you if you need help, but please allow yourself the time and space to heal and be whole.

CHAPTER 27

Going Home

When Perry graduated from high school, he followed in his dad's footsteps and took off for Alaska. His journey took him to Bristol Bay, Alaska, which, while famous for its own dangers, felt a safer choice than the Bering Sea, where Peter had worked. That experience gave birth to Perry's love for commercial fishing, and it was clear it was his passion and would be his future. It became clear to us as he committed to fishing for Dungeness crab with his dad's friend that he'd be making his home in Westport. In time we discussed the possibility of his buying my house. I'd tried to sell it a couple of times, but for a variety of reasons it just hadn't worked out, and I was at a point where I just needed to be done with it. I'd held on to it for so long because of the memories attached to it and, as with the boat, was fearful those memories would fade if I sold it.

It was the only home our kids had lived in with their dad, and the emotional attachment had prevented me from making sound decisions about it over the years. In a way, I think I hoped I'd eventually return to it myself. I loved where I was living, but it wasn't home for me, and I think I was holding out hope that moving back to my real home could happen. The time came, though, when I just had to let it go.

I didn't necessarily want Perry to buy the house. It was an old farmhouse with a mountain of issues that needed attention. The post and pier foundation needed some added support. The windows were still single pane, so the wind would seep its way into the home and remind the occupants that the original insulation was nothing more than old newspapers pasted to the interior of the walls. The upkeep of the home would be a lot for someone as young as Perry to manage. I was also hesitant to have him living in this house full of all the memories. So many good memories, but also so many filled with sadness and grief. I knew it would be something I'd need to deal with if he decided to live there. In time. Maybe . . .

He decided not to buy the house. He had other plans, so I proceeded to put it on the market. Literally, the day it was set to go live on the realtor's listing, Perry changed his mind and said he wanted it. Thank God for small towns and gracious realtors who are also friends! Our realtor worked with us so Perry could buy the house. I was apprehensive the first time we visited him after he moved in. I was steadying myself for the rush of emotions that would come flooding in. But instead, what I walked into was very much a bachelor pad and I was spared the emotional drain from stuffing the grief down yet again.

A couple of years later, Perry let go of the bachelor pad feel to welcome his son into the world and brought him home to that house full of memories. That was an incredibly significant moment for me, and it was then that the memories of being in that home with my own babies took me to my knees. It was then that my heart pulled me back to my home.

As soon as we learned that a baby was in our future, I yearned to be near this new precious gift and be a part of his life. I also felt a longing to be back with my hometown family and friends. I had a deep desire to be a present and active granny. I didn't want to be a long-distance grandparent. I wanted to be a down-the-road-stop-in-for-dinner grandparent. The type that can run up and just sit at the house while the baby is sleeping so Mom and Dad can go have a nice dinner. Or get called last minute to pick up kids from daycare. I wanted the impromptu family dinners and the stop in for a quick hug, and couldn't have that living three hours away.

All these thoughts swirled around in my head like my own personal tornado. I told Derek, "I really want to find a way to be in Westport more, but know our jobs and lives are here now."

He was kind in reassuring me. "We can spend as much time as our work schedule will allow in Westport, and in time we'll be retired and can spend as much time as we want then."

In that time, Sarah will be done with college and maybe she'll decide Westport will be her home as well. Then I can have all my babies with me.

We started to look for ways we could spend more time in Westport without intruding on family and their homes. We looked at property and houses we considered purchasing as our second home, when, one day, my realtor/silver-bookbag friend showed us a condo that suited our needs perfectly. We put in an offer, and it was accepted. Now we had a place we could stay in Westport that was out of the way and not intrusive to anybody.

I accepted Derek's response to my desire to be in Westport more often because it was true and felt like the wise approach to the situation. But even after we had the condo and could regularly visit, I still felt a restlessness in my soul like there was supposed to be something more. My heart wanted more. I felt myself wanting to be in Westport full-time. So, I went to God. I let him know my heart's desire and then I waited (not very patiently, mind you, because I reminded God every day of what I desired). Seven months later, He let me know He'd heard me.

◄o►

Perry had chosen commercial fishing as his career despite our efforts to convince him that other careers would be great options. He'd made a good effort to explore those options, but his heart kept being drawn back to fishing. I had a lot of respect for commercial fishermen, but wanted my son on land doing something safer. At twenty-two Perry bought his own commercial fishing boat, and at that point I knew he'd made up his mind. I set my feelings about the dangers of commercial fishing aside and supported him 100 percent. I'd rather he did something dangerous that made him happy than be safe and miserable.

The winter after Perry's son was born we made it a priority to be in Westport for Dump Day. Sounds weird and a bit like thirteen-year-old boy humor if you don't know what it is, right? Dump Day is the day commercial fishermen get to strategically lay ("dump") their crab pots in the ocean, signifying the official start of commercial Dungeness crab season. The days leading up are filled with hope and anticipation. The energy at the marina and around town is electrifying. There's an infectious excitement that's impossible to ignore. Many local families and businesses depend on a good crab season to sustain them for the entire year, so Dump Day is a big deal. We wanted to be there to support Perry and celebrate the start of the season with everyone.

That year started out different than years past. The start of the season had been delayed for a variety of reasons, and when the fishermen were finally allowed to go, some unusually cold winter weather came in and covered the area, including the marina, in a blanket of ice and snow. Ice on roads and driveways is difficult to navigate, but ice on a load of crab pots secured on the back deck of a boat is different. The additional weight as well as the risk of the load shifting while navigating the winter waters brought the dangers of the job to a much higher level.

The delay of a season is reason enough to raise concerns. The span of time from the last paycheck to the next becomes vast and people get anxious and tend to be more willing to take risks. They have families to feed and bills to pay and know their best opportunity for making money happens during a short window of time. The delay had already made the fishermen hungry to get started. The addition of bad weather created the potential for more risky decisions being made.

By the time we made it to the marina, the excitement was gone and a solemn air of caution had replaced it. News of a boat sinking that morning made the air thick with fear, adding an extra layer of caution that moved across the harbor like a marine layer cooling a hot summer day. Everywhere I turned I heard the same phrases being repeated: "Thankfully, all on board survived. Everyone survived. Nobody died." However, several other boats were experiencing dangerous situations that required assistance, and the distress calls being broadcast across VHF radios just heightened the already ominous feeling.

Making our way around the marina, we could see the feeling of apprehension. Nobody was smiling and those who were still at the dock were proceeding with great caution. This was one of the reasons I didn't want my son to be a commercial fisherman, and this was another reason why I wanted to move home. My heart felt a deep connection with each face I saw. This wasn't just a group of fishermen—this was my community, and I felt the strongest need to be a part of it again.

When the larger group of crabbers left the dock, we drove to the point to watch Perry's boat cross the bar and set out into the ocean. All the emotions from the day mixed with the fear I kept hidden behind a smile while encouraging those I encountered rested like a heavy weight on my chest. We sat watching the boats and prayed safety over each one as they crossed that bar. I prayed an extra prayer that my son would return safely and be spared any harm as I watched his boat disappear into a tiny speck along the horizon. I kept reminding myself, *No news is good news*. Thankful for how quickly technology had advanced since Peter was a fisherman, I was able to communicate with Perry throughout the day and receive the reassurance I needed that he was safe.

As we'd walked the marina earlier in the day, my attention was drawn to the two-story marina office and I became curious if anything new was happening in relation to the port. When we returned to the condo that afternoon, I visited the marina website to see what new projects might be coming. When I scrolled through the staff page I was brought directly to current job openings. I was surprised to see a job opening in the marina office that fitted me and my experience. Knowing this position hadn't come open in decades, it felt like a miracle opportunity that would allow me to transition back home. I shared the job posting with Derek, expecting him to say, "That's nice, but you have a job." Instead, he said, "That's perfect for you. You need to apply."

I was shocked. "Are you serious? Do you really think I should apply? It would mean I'd have to move here in order to work here. You understand that, right?"

"Yes, I completely understand that; and yes, I think you should apply for it. We already have a place to live here, and can make it work. Lots of couples make long distance work." I assumed we'd be moving back in a few years, not a few months, but God tends to not waste time when working out His plan.

Don't Worry—I Have a Plan.

"Okay, if you're sure, I'm going to go for it; and if it's meant to be, we'll make it work!" It sounded so easy.

I got the job, but making it work didn't go as smoothly as we had dreamed. Being apart wasn't as easy for us as it is for some, so Derek began looking for a job so he could move as well. Once again God worked it out, and Derek was hired into a position that has allowed him to live here and be a part of our family and community with about 90 percent less stress than his last job.

Moving back forced me to sort through the little stuffed box of grief I'd so carefully tucked away. I was finally coming full circle, and the emotions that greeted me were overwhelming at times. Obviously, I was excited to be moving home and getting the gift of being with family and being a present, active grandparent, but found myself worrying about how people might feel about my coming home. When I left, I did so in a bit of a hurry and my exit wasn't graceful. I don't do goodbyes well. I prefer to fade into the background and simply disappear. I left to keep a promise to Peter but with Perry and Sarah grown, I felt I'd kept my word, and my part of the agreement was satisfied. I wondered how to face all the people who'd loved and supported me through the darkest time of my life but with whom I'd lost contact after moving away. Would I even be welcomed back, and could I live in this small town in a private, quiet way?

I was also full of fear. While being fearful isn't a new thing for me, this time this fear was for much bigger reasons. I was fearful to face all the memories and emotions moving back might dredge up, which is part of why I needed to do this. I knew I needed to face it all. I was finding that spending more time in Westport was bringing old memories and old emotions to the surface that I'd carefully packed away for many years. Truthfully, I took pride in the fact that I could stuff my emotions in the deep well of my soul. So, having them slowly bubbling to the surface was, well, shocking at times. I realized that this gift of moving back home came with a price and that fee could be paid only by my facing my grief and doing some tough emotional work.

Going Home

When I gathered the courage to tell my boss that I'd got the job, he asked me a question that allowed me to answer with an honesty I hadn't been able to articulate until that moment.

"Stephanie, are you running away from something or are you running to something?"

I needed to make sure I was making this change for the right reasons. I looked at him and felt a fragility I hadn't felt in a very long time.

"I've been running away for a long time, and now I'm running toward what I need. I've been stuffing my emotions down for so long that I've run out of room to stuff. I need to go home. It's time for me to go home."

CHAPTER 28

Opening and Closing Wounds

I was prepared to face almost all the memories home would bring, but wasn't prepared for how these memories would present themselves. Walking the road of grief for so many years had taught me that memories could be triggered at random and unexpected times. I wished the unexpected part wasn't so prevalent.

I wasn't ready for the moment when I was waiting for my coffee at Captain Jack's and Peter's old friend Bill pulled up to the window on the other side of the coffee stand. He was someone we'd spent a lot of time with when we were dating. He was a kind person whom Peter referred to as "one of the good guys." I was comfortable with that simple memory playing in my mind while I waited for my coffee, until Bill made eye contact with me, smiled, and waved, and in an instant the flood of memories and emotion came over me in a way I wasn't prepared to handle. I gave a half-wave back, doing my best to look cheerful while fighting against the bombshell of emotions rising in my throat. Thankful my coffee was done, I grabbed it from the barista's hand and drove off just as the tears breached the emotional barricade I'd spent the last sixteen years constructing and tending to.

Those moments surprised me more than once. One evening we went out for a family dinner and sitting at a table adjacent to us was another of Peter's good friends with his family. The help he provided me after Peter passed away was immense and I never felt I was able to thank him properly. Even though I hadn't seen him in years, he was the type of guy I could call out of the blue if I needed help and he'd be there. I was happy to see him in the restaurant with his family, and waved and said hello from the next table over. I surprisingly became overwhelmed with emotion as I sat in my chair trying to focus on the menu. I looked at Derek and he asked, "Are you okay?" I nodded my head, but he could see my thoughts. "Do you need to give him a hug?" How did he know that was what I needed?

"Yeah, I do," I whispered. I knew this person had no idea how much his support for me and the kids after Peter died had meant to me. Even with tears in my eyes and words caught in my throat, I couldn't express my gratitude sufficiently. I could only hug him and hope he understood what I wanted to say but couldn't.

While difficult to work through at times, I learned that all these unexpected and uninvited emotional moments were slowly starting to heal me. I began to realize that all that stuffing down I'd done over the years, while allowing me to deal with life on the surface, hadn't allowed me to heal the hurt I was enduring deep in my soul. What I'd done over the years was send the grief and deep emotions into a hidden vault, perfectly preserved for me to deal with another time. That other time was what I ignorantly thought would be never. However, it turned out to be now. Being in my hometown, surrounded by all my memories, was forcing me to deal with all I was unwilling to address in the past. I was so focused on taking care of my kids and keeping my promises to Peter that I'd skillfully tucked my own deep grief away.

Maybe some of those people who questioned my grief timeline in the past weren't so inconsiderate after all or maybe it wasn't about the timeline but the way I chose to handle my emotions. Do I think I'd have chosen a different path had I taken things at a slower pace? No, I truly don't. I also believe I'd have found a way to stuff my grief down no matter how much time passed because I still find myself stuffing emotions instead of dealing with them today. Will I ever learn to manage my emotions in a healthy manner? I hope so. But I think I may spend the rest of my life learning how. And that's okay as long as I keep trying.

◄o►

I've learned that grief never leaves. It hangs around in the depths of your heart and mind waiting for an opportunity to remind you of the pain you still bear from loss. This hidden grief is especially prevalent when there's a new death. It doesn't necessarily have to be the death of a loved one. It could be the notice of a death of someone familiar, a mention of death on the news, or, in my case, most severely with the loss of a dog. Four years after losing Peter we had to say goodbye to our beloved Onyx. I felt all the buried emotions rise to the surface and take control once again. Then again, when we had to say goodbye to my Boxer six years after that, it was like the scab protecting my wounded heart was ripped away, allowing me to bleed my grief all over again. You may think you have a handle on your emotions. You've been down this road before, and this moment you're experiencing is so insignificant compared to what you've already experienced, yet it rips open the wounds of grief and brings a fresh flood of emotions that catches you off guard. It's okay to be in that moment and experience the emotions that have decided to reappear without your permission. In fact, I recommend you do. It's in these moments that you may wonder if you'll ever have control over your emotions and be able to navigate loss in a way that doesn't bring you to your knees. It's been over sixteen years since Peter's death, and I still don't handle loss well. I'm either emotionless and stone faced, guarding my heart with all my might, or a complete wreck and excusing myself to ugly cry in private. I don't think either of these reactions is wrong, but they aren't the graceful response I'd like to have.

I share this raw reality in hopes that it will bring comfort to someone who wonders if they're normal for continuing to fall apart or if they'll ever "be better" or "get over it." You may not and I think that's okay. Stop thinking something is wrong with you, because there isn't. You're okay to feel exactly what you're feeling. Just don't let this grief control your every-day life. Your loved one wouldn't want that for you.

Opening and Closing Wounds

I was gifted with knowing what Peter wanted for me and am forever thankful that God gave him the foresight to have that dreaded conversation with me. That conversation gave me the ability to move forward with living without questioning the big decisions. What I failed to show myself was grace while navigating the small obstacles. I wish I'd welcomed the peace that has come from working through my grief by facing some of my most painful memories earlier rather than stuffing them down for so many years. It's easy, though, to look back and see where you could have handled something differently. But in the moment, you do the best you can with what you have and that's what I did. My wish is that someone will learn from my experience and do better for themselves in their own journey.

CHAPTER 29

Imperfect Grief

I read a quote by an unknown author that stuck with me: "Don't forget you're human. It's okay to have a meltdown. Just don't unpack and live there. Cry it out and then refocus on where you're headed." I appreciate this quote because it reminds me I'm allowed to pause in my grief and acknowledge my emotions, but doing so doesn't mean I need to stop and stay in that place forever. I can feel the emotions but then move on to better feelings and brighter destinations.

This quote also reinforces that there are no real rules for grief—it's done in your way and in your time. You may have times when you carry yourself well on the outside, but are still falling apart on the inside, and in the eyes of others have gotten over it. It's okay if inside you're still grieving. Just because others can't see your pain doesn't mean it isn't there or it isn't real. There's no requirement to share how you're feeling with others if you don't feel inclined to do so. I kept a lot to myself for many years in an attempt to protect not only myself but also those around me. I believed that if I kept moving forward, I'd come out the other side better; and if I kept the pain to myself, I could protect those around me from feeling the pain as well. That isn't true. Keeping your pain from those who love you only hurts you and your relationship with them.

Healing from grief can take a lifetime. Literally, a lifetime. People will tell you that in time you'll get over your grief and they'll remind you there are five or seven steps in the grief process and all you need to do is get through all the steps and you'll be better. Of course, just like following a recipe. Start with some sadness and heartache, add a little denial and anger, throw in some bargaining and depression, and top it off with my favorite: acceptance. Simple little steps to follow and move on. Easy.

If only it were that easy.

I knew of other women in my community who'd lost their husbands, but didn't have the emotional strength to reach out to them. I wanted so badly to talk to them and be reassured that I could do this. That I'd make it through and survive. I understand now why they didn't reach out. It's not easy seeing the grief you've experienced on someone else's face. It brings it all back to the surface as though it has just happened, and that pain can be excruciating. I've found myself learning of women who've lost their husbands and wanted to reach out to them, but have held back many times because I fear the pain I know it will cause me. I've vowed over and over to be better but have often failed. I'm hopeful that sharing my story now will help others who are searching for the validation of their emotions, the fear of what comes next, and the hope and confidence that they'll be okay.

This is a grief carried for life and while it may not always consume you as it did in the beginning, it's always there ready to pop up at a moment's notice when a memory is triggered, or a smell or sound takes you back. Standing in the middle of the busy grocery store during the holidays, I burst into tears and was borderline hysterical because there was eggnog. It reminded me of Peter pretending to sneak eggnog milkshakes upstairs after Perry and Sarah were already tucked in bed. "Shhh . . . don't tell your mom or we'll all get into trouble." The sounds of delightful giggles drifted down to me, exposing their secret pact and warming my heart. It all played back as I stood staring at the dairy display in front of me. People looked at me standing there in my grief, but nobody said a word. In that moment, I could have used a "Hey, are you okay?" I could have shared my little story and turned that moment into one of healing instead of pain and sadness.

Think of this when you see someone having a moment and wonder if you should say something or keep moving on. Just stop and ask if they need something. If they tell you to mind your own business, do just that and keep moving along. However, there's a chance you could give someone an incredible gift of just showing them someone cares.

You may never be able to fully relieve yourself of this grief but, in time, you can learn to experience these memories and moments in a way that makes you smile and feel grateful to have them. In the end, you'd rather have painful memories than none at all.

Grief and the fear of loss are something you carry with you into future parts of your life in unexpected ways. As hard as I fight it, I find myself checking on Derek at random times in the night to make sure he's breathing. Most days of the week I hold my breath waiting/hoping he'll wake up in the mornings. I outwardly celebrated our ninth wedding anniversary, but inwardly prayed fervently he wouldn't drop dead that day. I think I even thanked him for not dying! Every time he gets into the car or on his motorcycle, I wait for a phone call notifying me he's been in an accident. I know it's unhealthy and irrational, and when the thoughts creep in I have to interrupt them. I continually find myself praying that one day I can be at peace with life the way it is and not live in constant fear of losing another husband.

I worry about my kids and their future. I see my son, who has started his own family now, and pray that his following in our footsteps stops at the boat, house, and his family and that he leads a long and happy life. I'm unable to concentrate on normal tasks when my daughter is driving thirteen hours over three passes in the snow. I'm thankful for today's technology and that she shares her location with me so I can watch her little car figure move across the map on my phone. I pray that my children can live their lives without any further experiences of unexpected, tragic loss.

I worry that maybe I didn't do enough to emotionally support my kids. Yes, we went to counseling, and not just when they were younger. I took them again when they were older, but always feel I could have done more. I desired to teach them that although we'd had a terrible, tragic event in our lives, we were strong and, with God's strength and grace, would make it through. We weren't going to be the victims who'd always be labeled as the family who lost their husband or dad. I wanted to teach them to not wallow but acknowledge and live forward.

In my desire to protect them, I worry I might have overlooked opportunities to teach them how to have healthy conversations about their emotions. They reassure me I'm a great mom and I know they love me, but I wish I could have given them the time and space to feel their emotions more honestly with me.

I hid so much from my loved ones, and especially my children. I didn't let them see me grieve the real raw grief. I did my best to hide that from them because I thought if they saw it, it would scare them or they'd see me as a weak victim, and I refused to raise them as victims. I remember sitting at my kitchen table a few days after Peter died and some extremely loving women from my church were visiting. There were several kids in the house, and my son quietly came to my side and asked if they could go outside and play. "Of course, you can," I said. "Just be careful and be nice to each other." They all ran out to the yard and started climbing on the play structure.

As soon as they all got out the door, I fell apart, dropping my head into my hands and sobbing. In the midst of my breakdown, I felt gentle hands on my arms, causing me to look up, begging for an answer: "I don't know what to do. What am I supposed to do?" If there was a reply, I didn't hear it over my own cries. I do know these women gathered around me and prayed for me and my children. I know the love they poured over me in that moment was all I needed. They just sat with me and let me have my moment without offering advice I couldn't hear, instruction I couldn't follow, or food I couldn't eat. They just loved me through it, and I wish I'd given my kids the gift of witnessing those moments.

It's not easy to look back and see the areas I could have done better, but it's necessary because doing so may give someone else the confidence or permission to walk their path a little differently, and maybe their journey through grief will be just a little bit easier because of this.

Don't Worry—I Have a Plan.

◄○►

I tried so hard to not let this one tragic moment define me. I didn't want to be known as Stephanie the Widow. I wanted to just be me and not have this tagline attached to my identity. But over the years and through the process of writing this book, I've realized it's *my* identity, and I'm okay with being known as Stephanie the Widow because I'm doing well. I have an amazing life and I want other people who've lost their spouse to see they can survive the grief and still live a lovely life. I want others to see it's possible to live through heartbreak like I did and still be able to live forward while honoring your loved one.

I'm okay now with saying Peter's tragic death defined me—because it did. It changed my approach to everything in life. My life was blown up and, as it landed like little fragments of shrapnel all around me, I became purposeful in which pieces I picked up and how I allowed those pieces to be placed back together. I left a lot of pieces lying on the ground and, over time, went back and picked some of them up. But a lot of them I left because they just didn't feel as important as they once did, and they didn't fit with the life we were now living.

It has defined how I approach life and it has been a measurement for many life moments. When something tough happens, I think, *Well, it isn't as bad as losing a husband* or *I've experienced worse* or *Life does go on.* My instant thought is, *Did anybody die?* If not, then whatever the situation, we can deal with it.

◄○►

I was given four incredible gifts that helped me through the storm.

First, God gave me that dream about Peter's dying, which was no coincidence. It was a gift I was able to tell Peter about and have him spell out in detail what he wanted me to do if something were to happen to him. That kept me from spending the rest of my life alone and always asking the question "Would Peter be okay with this?" I knew how to live forward with making decisions because he'd told me what he wanted for me and our children.

The second gift was my children. They kept me alive. I got up every day and made it through each painful moment because of them. They were the reason I didn't curl up in bed and die right along with Peter—because that's what I wanted to do. I got up each day, asked God for help, put on my best face, and dealt with everything as it came because they needed me. They needed their mom to be there for them and, while I know I failed them in many ways, I hope they know they were my reason for living.

The third gift was the ability to love again. The gift of Derek as my husband has given me the ability to live forward. His patience with me through the years of sporadic grieving, accepting my and Peter's family as his own, and his love for Perry and Sarah is more than I could have dreamed of receiving. We might not have done it all well but, with God's grace, have done it together.

The fourth and most impactful was that small, simple message that has carried the most powerful promise ever given to me: "Don't worry - I have a plan." Thank you, God, for meeting me in my most fragile moment to give me your promise. You took tragedy and turned it into something beautiful. I know your promise was never to spare us from pain, but that, if we allow you to, you'll turn our mourning into dancing, and have done just that. I've clung to this promise every time I've worried, questioned my circumstances, or doubted my discernment of life decisions. Your plan isn't over, but what you've done so far is more than my human brain or heart could ever have imagined. I can't wait to see what you have in store for us next!

There's a lot of debate regarding who God is—some almighty deity sitting in heaven making sure we're following the rules and waiting to rain down his wrath. Or someone looking upon us with the love and grace of a true father ready to pick us up when we fall and love us through our struggles. When I think of God, I think of my story. I think of how He carried me. He was there when I was swept away by the wave as a child, and he was there decades later when my world crumbled around me. He carried me through every straggled breath, sleepless night, and moments of self-doubt. He held me in my most fragile moments and gave me the strength I needed when I didn't think I could put one foot in front of the other. He guided me through my mourning and set me on a path of healing. If He can bring me through this most horrific event, then He can bring me through anything else that comes my way. Not that I'm inviting anything else, but I stand with confidence knowing I can release all control and will be just fine.

I don't know what His complete plan is or when it will come to fruition. But as I look back on my life and see how certain events have unfolded to this point, I'm eternally grateful for His love and grace. I've been able to look back through my story and see how God prepared me for this moment. All the decisions, conversations, and significant life events leading to this tragic loss where I was given a promise tell me there is a plan and more good things are to come.

What if the purpose for my life from the beginning was to experience this tragic loss so I could one day retell it to you in a way that encourages you in your own situation or provides you with a bit of hope so you can face whatever difficulties you're experiencing? What if my purpose was to provide you with the validation that while your experience feels more difficult than you think you can bear, you're still here, and my story can give you the courage to keep living forward?

Whatever the reason, my prayer is that my story will encourage you to seek the hope in your own.

Full Circle

Thanksgiving 2022, gathered with family in my son's home, enjoying the smell of warm turkey, stuffing, and all the delicious side dishes, I stand to the side of the room observing all that's happening around me. My daughter is here, and my parents have joined us as well as my daughter-in-love, Mikayla, and her family. As I look around this home filled with family, love, and laughter, I'm taken back twenty years to a Thanksgiving I hosted in this same space.

I see myself tending to the turkey as it finishes in the oven and asking my dad if he'd carve it when it's ready. Today, Mikayla is watching the turkey and has just quietly asked her dad if he'd carve it when it's ready. We had a table set with appetizers to keep the hungry people satisfied until dinner was served and, when it was time, moved it to a side table to make room for the main dishes. Now, Perry and Mikayla are skillfully rearranging appetizer dishes and making room for the completed Thanksgiving meal. Sarah is entertaining my grand babies, Cohen and sweet Ada Bay, as Peter's sister did so long ago with Perry and Sarah. Perry retreats to visit with Derek, my dad, and the grandparents in the same living room where Peter engaged in conversation with family so many years before.

I remember feeling like there wasn't enough room to host everyone in this house, but loading the kids up and taking them elsewhere was more work than cramming everyone in this space and cooking the food here.

Don't Worry—I Have a Plan.

My now-adult son walks by: "Mom, we need a bigger house. There isn't enough room for everyone here."

I smile at the connection across time. "There's plenty of room here. Nobody is wanting for more. This house has been accommodating gatherings like this one for years." He raises his eyebrows and smiles as he sets up a second table for food.

As the movement continues like a well-choreographed performance, I drift between the memories of so long ago when Peter and I were raising our babies in this home and today, when Perry and Mikayla are raising theirs.

Sarah, who was the baby being doted over by grandparents and aunties, is now the auntie doting over her nephew and niece. Soon there's a shift in the air, and with the rising temperature from the oven working overtime and the extra bodies in close proximity, people start feeling the effects of the warmth paired with full tummies. Some decide it's time to take leave so they can nap and enjoy leftovers in their own home. Like clockwork, my mom takes her beloved spot at the kitchen sink and gets to work cleaning up from a full day of cooking and serving, and does her best to shoo Mikayla away. "Go sit down and rest. You've done so much already." I'm instantly taken back to Thanksgivings of the past when my mom tried to shoo me away so she could clean up.

Like a slow-motion reel in a movie, my two Thanksgivings with twenty years between them overlap in front of me. I watch as my two worlds meld together as one, and know God has given me this moment to show me all He has done for me. For my family. I hear a whisper . . . "Don't worry - I have a plan." As I'm allowed to experience this full-circle moment and acknowledge how far we've come, I'm overwhelmed with gratitude for this gift of seeing my beautiful family as we were in the past, happy and content, and now, whole and happy again.

Things I Learned

Over the years, I've been asked how to help someone who has just experienced a loss. I wouldn't call myself an expert by any means, but having lived through a loss, I do have some thoughts or suggestions from my own experience. None of these are fail-safe and there are a million more acts of service one can provide, but these are a few options for someone searching for a way to help comfort someone they care about.

WHAT YOU MIGHT WANT TO SAY

I think many people struggle with knowing what to say or how to help a person or family who has experienced a tragic loss like mine. I understand how hard it is to know what to say in these situations. I still find myself struggling for the right words, and I've lived through it. As I mentioned earlier, the head tilt, sad face, and "I'm so sorry. How are you doing?" can feel tiresome after being asked a multitude of times. I know everyone who says it means the best, and it's an expression of sympathy, but it's nice to get asked something different. Something that evokes a more sincere answer than a surface emotion. That isn't a negative statement against anyone expressing sympathy—it can just be difficult to hear it over and over again.

The "How are you doing?" question is one we tend to blurt out. I asked it recently of someone who'd just lost their spouse. As soon as the words came out of my mouth, I wished I could pull them back. I looked at this friend and, shaking my head, said, "I'm so sorry. I know exactly how you're doing and it's not well. Please forgive me for asking such a surface question." As he nodded his head with understanding, I rephrased and asked, "Where are you in your grief, and is there anything I can do to support you?"

Again, it's not a bad question. Just be thoughtful about asking it if you do and be open and ready for whatever answer you get from the person you're asking. You may be met with a Snarky Stephanie, who blurts back, "Obviously, I'm great!" Just be patient and don't take anything personally. The emotions of grieving are unpredictable at best.

I can't speak for everyone, but can speak for myself and a few others I've had the privilege of talking to over the years. There are so many other ways to express sympathy instead of "I'm sorry."

While "sorry" feels appropriate, you could try something like: *My heart hurts for you. I'm here for you if you need me. I can just sit here with you if you like. We don't have to talk, but I can just be with you.* Allowing someone to draw from your strength during a time when they have none is one of the greatest gifts you can give. Words are not always necessary. Most of the time your presence in a time of sorrow is all that's needed. *I know I can't make this better for you, but I'm here and willing to support you in the way you need. I understand you may not know how to express what you're feeling right now, but if you need to talk, I'm here for you.*

There are so many options. If you know the person well enough to show up at their house or the service honoring their loved one, then trust your gut when offering them support. Sometimes no words are necessary, but a kind act speaks volumes.

WHAT YOU CAN DO

One of the questions I get asked the most is, "What can I do?" People stand before me feeling lost about how to help their loved one when tragedy has struck. The conversation we then have reveals to me how uncomfortable people are not only with death itself but with the surviving widow/widower/partner. I understand this. I can recall the many times I've stood frozen in place trying to figure out how to help the survivor—and *I'm* one! I've spent countless hours mulling this over in my head, talking to people who walked beside me during my time of loss, and reading articles and books about dealing with loss, and the conclusion I keep coming up with is the same: no matter the circumstances, the best thing to do is acknowledge how horrible the situation is and just tell them you're there for them. And then be there for them.

Ask yourself what the grieving person may need. Do they need help with housework? Do they need lawn care? Do they have kids who need help getting to T-ball or soccer practice? Or maybe they need help picking them up after school? Do they need groceries or help with meal prep? Or do they just need someone to sit next to them in silence so they can have the most precious gift of knowing they aren't traveling this road alone?

If you don't have the answer to this question, ask them. If they say they don't know, which is a very acceptable answer, offer to do some menial, daily task like taking out the trash, dusting, or washing dishes to take at least one thing off their plate and mind.

Sometimes just knowing you're not alone means the most. When you've lost your spouse, partner, and best friend, you could have a million people all around you, but the world has suddenly become the loneliest place you've ever experienced. All it takes is for one person to reach for your hand to remind you you're not alone.

Don't give up on the person grieving. If you offer your assistance and get turned down, don't take it personally, and don't take that as the final answer. Someone who's grieving doesn't always know what they may need or want at any given moment. Allow them time to breathe and then offer again. Obviously, if they continue to turn you down after several offers, you should just stop offering or say, "Hey, I understand this may not be the time you need me, but if you change your mind there's no expiration date on this. I'll be around and ready to help when you need me." Then you wait for that person to reach out.

There's nothing wrong with reminding them after some time has passed (such as three or six months, or even longer), "Hey, don't forget. I'm here for you. No expiration. Open-ended." Then go about your business. They may never reach out and that's okay. But they may surprise you and one day eight months later call saying, "Remember that offer to help? I'm feeling really overwhelmed with cleaning out closets. Would you mind helping for an hour or two?" Say yes and make it happen! That might have been extremely difficult for them to ask. So, unless they're requesting something illegal or physically impossible for you to do, show up and do it!

The gift of your assistance, and mostly your presence, is a gift that goes far beyond the surface level and is one the griever's heart will never forget. This may not be revolutionary advice for many of you, and may seem very simple, but in times of grief, simple is good. These are just basic guidelines for helping and can be a good foundation to start from. The options are endless and, many times, how your help is needed depends on the person in need. Don't be afraid to reach out and don't be offended if your offer isn't accepted. Sometimes just knowing someone cares is enough to comfort the griever.

Thank You Isn't Enough

How do you thank the people who've prompted, encouraged, and given support through a long and an incredibly emotional journey? How do you show appropriate appreciation for those who picked you up when the floor dropped out from beneath you? There are no words adequate to thank everyone who has shown me so much love and support. I've tried to do so with my heart in this book and hope as you've read it you've felt it.

First, I thank God for being with me in my darkest moment. I'm eternally grateful for those words whispered to me, giving me the strength I needed to carry on. Thank you, Jesus, for going before me and setting my path for me. As the psalmist wrote, *My life is an example to many, because you have been my strength and protection* (Psalm 71:7 NLT).

Perry and Sarah, you lived this journey with me, and I know how difficult it is to relive it through the words on these pages, so I thank you from the depths of my soul for allowing me to follow God's direction and see this to completion. God carried me through the loss but you two kept me alive. You two precious souls were what motivated me to keep taking each breath and helped me put one foot in front of the other day after day. I'm in awe of the amazing people you've become. You're my greatest accomplishment. My love for you knows no bounds.

Derek, my love. Your willingness to partner with me through this life has meant everything to me. I know there are parts of this journey that have been difficult. We have traveled to the bottom of the pit and climbed our way back up to the top, and have done it together with God's help. Thank you for believing in me when I didn't believe in myself. Thank you for your honesty, your love, your kindness, and compassion.

Don't Worry—I Have a Plan.

You were a gift to me seventeen years ago and you're still a gift to me now. I love you with all my heart.

My parents, Randy and Yoyo, you've always been there for me when I needed you and have supported me through each of life's challenges. You're my biggest cheerleaders, and I thank you for always believing in and encouraging me to keep going. You've given me so much more than I deserve, and I'll never take that for granted.

Scott and Trisha, my incredible brother and sweet sister-in-law. The gift of your love and friendship means everything to me. Scott, the strength you showed when I asked you to relay the most devastating news to Peter's mom amazes me every time I recall that day. I asked you to do the worst job ever and you didn't even blink an eye. You did it for your sister who desperately needed you in that moment. I can't imagine a world without my big brother in it. Trisha, you were and continue to be Scott's rock and your love and support for me throughout the years is immeasurable. I love you both so much.

Pat, Teresa, and Molly, it was your words that prompted this journey. God knew I needed prompting. Pat and Teresa, you encouraged me to write my story and, with every prompt, I met you with total obstinance. When I silently made a bargain with God that if He sent a third person unassociated with my past to say the words "You should write a book," Molly, you had no idea you'd be that voice, but I'm so glad you were. If you hadn't spoken those words, this book wouldn't exist. Thank you all for accepting the task of praying for and encouraging me through this journey.

Andrea, Malynnda, Mandy, and Tina, you encouraged and prayed and listened to me when I said I couldn't do it. You showed me compassion when I was struggling and kicked my butt when I was procrastinating. You were there for me in my darkest hours. You held me when I cried and, when I had no words to share, sat with me and allowed me to draw from your strength. Thank you for being my forest, LULAS.

Julie, my longest, loving, friend. No time that passes diminishes our bond. You're always here for me and my kids and it just isn't fair how selflessly you give when there's no amount of time adequate to allow me to repay you. You tell me I give equally to this friendship, but I just don't see how that can be because what I get from you most certainly outweighs what you get from me. You're such a gift.

Aunt Patty and Uncle Jeff, your willingness to read my raw material and see the potential when I saw none became the encouragement I needed to not toss it aside and try to forget this project. Your heart and wisdom are unparalleled. I love you so much.

To those who've been named in this book, please know that your name has been included because you played a vital part in my story and healing. I've held close to my heart how you impacted my life and this journey. Thank you.

Andrea Ramsay (developmental editor), Eldo Barkhuizen (five-star copyeditor/proofreader extraordinaire), Darcie Clemons (editor), Taylor Hughes (not-your-average magician/author/publishing coach), Bob Goff (author/encourager/overall inspiration), thank you for sharing your knowledge and expert advice with me. Without your guidance, I wouldn't have known where to begin or finish this work of the heart. Thank you!

◄○►

You have turned my mourning into joyful dancing. You have taken away my clothes of mourning and clothed me with joy, that I might sing praises to you and not be silent. O Lord my God, I will give you thanks forever! (Psalm 30:11–12 NLT)

Made in United States
Troutdale, OR
01/06/2025

27587543R10123